The Beginner's Guide to
the Gift of Prophecy

The Beginner's Guide to the Gift of Prophecy

JACK DEERE

SERVANT PUBLICATIONS
ANN ARBOR, MICHIGAN

Vine Books is an imprint of Servant Publications especially designed to serve evangelical Christians.

All Scripture quotations, unless otherwise indicated, are taken from the HOLY BIBLE, NEW INTERNATIONAL VERSION®. Copyright 1973, 1978, 1984 by International Bible Society. Used by permission of Zondervan Publishing House. All rights reserved.

Published by Servant Publications
P.O. Box 8617
Ann Arbor, Michigan 48107

Cover design: Alan Furst

01 02 03 04 10 9 8 7 6 5 4 3

Printed in the United States of America
ISBN 1-56955-204-5

LIBRARY OF CONGRESS CATALOGING-IN-PUBLICATION DATA

Deere, Jack
The beginner's guide to the gift of prophecy / Jack Deere.
        p. cm.
    Includes bibliographical references.
    ISBN 1-56955-204-5 (alk. paper)
    1. Prophecy–Christianity. 2. Deere, Jack. I. Title.

BR115.P8 D44 2001
234'.13–dc21   00-049440

Dedication

For Rick and Julie Joyner,
faithful friends who have done more
than anyone I know to restore
prophetic ministry to the church.

Contents

Preface / 9

Acknowledgments / 11

1. Nobody Ever Told Me / 13
2. Discovering Your Gift / 27
3. Learning How God Reveals / 43
4. Discerning God's Voice / 63
5. Understanding God's Meaning / 81
6. Avoiding Prophetic Craziness / 103
7. Giving Prophetic Messages / 113
8. Deceptions, Demons, and False Prophets / 129
9. Growing in Your Prophetic Gift / 143

Postscript: Enjoying the Symphony / 157

Recommended Reading About Prophetic Ministry / 159

Preface

This book is a practical guide to contemporary prophetic ministry, not a scholarly monograph. A large part of the book is a telling of my own prophetic experience or my own encounters with the prophets, and also a telling of Paul Cain's story. Paul is the most accomplished prophet I know. I have learned a great deal about the prophetic ministry simply by observing him over the years, and I want you to profit from his experience as well.

I have attempted to support all the experiences and guidelines offered in the book with clear scriptural statements. In the few places where I could not find unambiguous biblical support for something common in contemporary prophetic ministry, I have tried to indicate that.

I hope no one will be offended by the masculine tone of the book. I have used the word "prophet" almost exclusively for two reasons. First, most of the biblical examples deal with prophets rather than prophetesses. Second, writing "prophet or prophetess" throughout the book would have been both cumbersome and tiresome. I hope the reader will be able to discern from the stories in the book the high esteem in which I hold prophetic women.

Finally, this book only tells the personal part of prophetic ministry, the basics to help you get started. Lord willing, I intend to follow this book with another on how and why the prophetic ministry must be integrated into the whole ministry of the church as we move further down the road of the last days.

Acknowledgments

Special thanks go to Ken Gire, my friend and one of the most skillful writers I know, who read the entire manuscript and offered many valuable suggestions. I also have the proud father's pleasure of thanking my son, Stephen Craig Deere, an award-winning journalist, who also made significant improvements to this book with his own deft touch. And finally, thanks to the wonderful folks at Servant, especially Kathy Deering, my editor.

Acknowledgments

ONE

Nobody Ever Told Me

D id God bring me here, or did the devil bring me here—
into this room to face someone I had never met, who
knew my painful secrets? My façade of indifference was being
assaulted secret by secret. Or was my heart being healed secret
by secret? Was this torture or surgery? What good could possibly come from reading aloud the pages in a book of pain that I
had closed forever? Yet it was I who had given the prophet permission to begin, and now I could not stop him.

Nobody ever told me prophets were like this. Until that day,
I had never met a prophet outside the pages of the Bible. I did
not believe prophets existed outside the pages of the Bible.
Because we have the Bible, I could not see why we needed
prophets. Besides, if we let them run loose outside the Bible,
who could predict the chaos they might cause? To me, the
prophets were just a temporary substitute for the real thing, the
Bible.

Then something happened to change my view. But that is
another story, which I tell in another book, *Surprised by the
Power of the Spirit*. Let me just say that I found more reasons to
believe in the existence of the prophets than to believe God had
set them aside. But what did I believe? I still had a mostly theo-
retical belief. Then I heard from a friend that there were

prophets, *real* prophets, in Kansas City. He was going to meet them. Would I like to go with him?

I called my spiritual mentor to tell him I was going to meet these prophets. At the other end of the line I pictured his face frowning, his brow wrinkling as he said, "Jack, don't let them deceive you. God gave you a mind. Remember to use it." I knew no one more experienced in the supernatural ministry of the Holy Spirit than my mentor. I knew no one with a kinder spirit. And he **was** skeptical. His warning transformed my excitement about meeting these prophets into a shield of determination not to be deceived.

But my shield would not protect me. From the moment I decided to go to that meeting I was doomed. Not because I was about to face an onslaught of controversy. Not because I would spend countless hours defending a ministry maligned by many church leaders. And not even because I would spend more hours binding up the wounds of prophetic abuses. I was doomed because I would never again be happy in church or ministry unless it was infused with the power of prophecy. The mind God had given me was no match for the prophetic heart.

So, on a bright sunny September afternoon, with my biblically guarded heart and skeptical mind, I met Mike Bickle, the pastor of these prophets and of the church, which then was called Kansas City Fellowship. Mike was not very tall, yet he was built like one of those halfbacks who got so sick of being told he was too small to play football that he disappeared into the weight room and when he came out he ran over a thousand bigger tacklers on his way to winning the Heisman Trophy. His deep voice resonated with authority. Above all, he radiated joy. In his presence, I felt joyful, too. I could not imagine him ever having a down day. Before I knew it, I was disarmed and charmed. I wanted Mike's joy, and his passion for God.

But the joy did not last past the next morning. When I awoke, I remembered that I had come to meet prophets, not pastors. Before breakfast, I traded my joy for a superior attitude that was determined not to be deceived. I finished my last gulp of coffee, wiped my napkin across my mouth, and was ready to meet these so-called prophets.

That morning when my wife Leesa and I arrived at the church, we were led into a dingy little room with green carpet and orange plastic chairs arranged in a circle. Five friends had come with us. They wanted to encounter God. I wanted to evaluate men. Mike and four new faces were waiting for us. The first of those new faces met me at the door.

He was a six-footer with an athletic build, dressed as if he had just walked out of an Eddie Bauer catalogue. His face, though, was the kind of face you would expect to see on someone more at home in a camel hair tunic and sandals. He had longish gray-ing hair, a salt-and-pepper beard, and disturbing, deep-set eyes. The eyes made him look otherworldly.

At first I thought his eyes were evil.

Then I couldn't make up my mind.

Then he spoke.

"Oh, I didn't expect to see you here this morning."

Pretty cocky, I thought. Already I did not like him. "What do you mean? I don't even know you," I said.

"Well *I* know you. It was eight nights ago. I had a dream. I woke up at three in the morning. I thought it was important so I wrote it down. You were in the dream. Would you like me to tell you what the Lord showed me about you?"

"Yes," is what I said. What I thought was, *Try me. Take your best shot. I'm not going to be deceived. I have been warned about you prophets.* I should mention that I was in a completely different tradition of Christianity than this fellow, and he really did not know me.

We took our seats in the circle. I knew about "cold reading," a skill used by gamblers, palm readers, and probably by false prophets as well. By careful observation of your clothing, expressions, and mannerisms skilled people can "read" you without knowing you. For example, a fortune-teller might notice pet hair on your clothes and say, "My spirit guide tells me you love animals." A gambler might notice that just before a man bluffs in a hand of poker, he always sighs. Gamblers call these signs "tells" because they tell something about you. Cold readers are also skillful in getting you to admit the details of your life in a way that makes it look like those details have been supernaturally revealed to them. On this morning, I knew that no matter how skilled in the art of deception this guy might be, I would give him no signs to read, no tells to help him win this game. I hardened my face like stone. We stared straight into each other's eyes. My eyes revealed nothing. Then he spoke, and revealed everything.

"You have a prayer," he said in a soft southern accent, "but it's more than a prayer. It's one of the major dreams of your heart." Then he told me the prayer I had prayed that very morning in the hotel. It was a prayer I prayed almost every morning. And he was right. It *was* the dream of my heart.

"God said to tell you this dream is from him and you will get what you're asking for."

I could tell you what the prayer was and still is, but telling it now would be, at the very least, immodest, and worse, perhaps self-serving. At the time, it was the biggest thing I could think to ask for. And here, like Daniel, is this prophet telling me my dream and that it will come true.

My granite face did not crack, not even slightly. My eyes remained placid, not a flicker of joy. He was getting no clues from me. But inside, my heart was exploding with joy. I had not cried since I was twelve years old. It took a superhuman effort not to cry now. Until that moment, I had never understood the expression "tears of joy." Why would anyone, especially a man, want to cry when he was happy? Maybe I had never been happy enough to know until now. How could I be so special to God that he would put such a dream in my heart and then tell me he would make it happen?

Next subject.

"You had a father who dropped the ball on you," he said. No! Not my father. That subject was off limits. Decent people never brought it up. How could he know about my father? My interior supports were giving way. How could he talk so calmly about the defining pain of my life? How could I hold it together any longer? If I let out what I was feeling now, I might destroy the self I had worked so long and hard to build. These fears kept me staring blankly at the prophet.

My father had dropped the ball on me, on all of us. One morning we woke up a normal middle-class family of six, ready for a normal day. I went along with my two little brothers and my baby sister to play at our grandmother's house. Mom went to work at her insurance office. My father stayed at home. By mid-morning, the lines for my father's last battle had formed in his soul. We never saw it coming. Sometime that afternoon, in the living room of our little three-bedroom house, my father put a gun to his head and ended the war raging within him. That night my mother went to bed alone, a thirty-four-year-old widow with an eleventh-grade education and four small children to raise. We would never be a normal family again.

I was the oldest of the kids. I had just turned twelve. Beyond some friends who brought the customary meals, there was no one to help us understand or heal.

My father had been my hero, my image of what it meant to be a man. He was strong and he was smart. Life without him was unimaginable. That is probably why I never really grieved. In order to grieve you have to face the reality of your loss, and that was too scary for me. No one was there to tell me that you couldn't heal *unless* you grieve. God was there, but it never occurred to me to pray to him. He wouldn't give me my father back. So what was the use of asking? Pain and confusion puddled in the bottom my heart. I never troubled those dark waters again. I stepped around them with a vow to be strong, never to need anyone again.

That reservoir of pain, hidden from me by my vow, did what all unhealed pain eventually does—it turned into bitterness. Long after I had ceased to feel the pain, the bitterness, which I could not feel, fueled all kinds of wild and shameful behavior.

At seventeen, the Lord reined me in before I killed myself trying to gain the admiration of my friends with the next tour de force of recklessness. Overnight, I became a follower of Jesus. Overnight, I lost my wild ways and wayward friends. But I did not lose the reservoir of bitterness. Still ignorant of its presence, I did not even know to talk about it to Jesus.

Nobody ever told me about bitterness. Or about the anger

born of bitterness and how it was behind my former rebellion and immorality. Nobody ever told me that even after you become a Christian, bitterness does not go away automatically. Nobody ever told me that bitterness hidden in your heart can make you skeptical of the goodness in others, even skeptical of God's goodness toward you. Nobody ever told me that bitterness can make you afraid to love too much for fear you will be cheated again.

Nobody ever told me that if you leave the bitterness alone, it will integrate itself so perfectly into your personality that you won't even know it's there and that you will end up dealing with the symptoms of your anger and harshness but never with their cause. People had told me that the sins of your youth come back to haunt you. But nobody ever told me that the bitterness of your youth can hound you all the way to the grave.

By the time I was thirty-eight years old, since no one else had told me, Jesus decided it was time he told me about these things. He started by talking to me about the death of my father, the time when the spiritual acid first began to pool in my twelve-year-old heart. And he sent this preppy prophet with the strange eyes into this dingy room to begin the conversation. At that moment, I had no idea what the Lord was doing. I wasn't even sure it *was* the Lord. All I knew was what I could feel, the prophet assaulting me with my own secrets, bringing up something wrong that could never be made right. I wanted the conversation to end. But the soft southern voice continued.

"The Lord is going to make up the loss of your father to you. He will send you new fathers. You won't learn from just one man. You will have the father you need for each new stage in your life."

Bringing up my father's death pained me, but the promise of new fathers bewildered me. How could anyone, even God, make up for the loss of a twelve-year-old boy's father? I didn't need new fathers. I was thirty-eight years old. I *was* a father myself. And I was totally happy with the spiritual mentor who was then in my life. I couldn't imagine I would ever need anyone else. But I said none of this aloud. I just returned his words with an unflinching stare.

Next subject.

"When you were young, the Lord gave you athletic ability, but he allowed you to be frustrated in the use of it. This was so you would put all your effort into cultivating the intellect. You've done that, but it hasn't brought you what you expected, and you're heartsick."

He could not have given a more accurate synopsis of the past thirty-eight years.

I was born with athletic ability. I was strong and quick. In Little League baseball I could play every position on the field and always batted in the top four. I grew up playing tackle football with no pads on. Then, when it was time to start seventh grade, the time when I could play organized sports for the school, I lost my father. Everything changed.

There was no one to take me to practices or to bring me home. My mother worked late into the evenings, selling insurance and collecting premiums to keep her four little kids fed and clothed and under one roof. Sports were not on her list of necessities. I learned how to make the evening meals, and I missed out on the next three years of sports.

Sports were the most important thing in life to me, not just because I enjoyed them more than anything else, but because if you were a guy in Texas in the early 1960s, it was the way you proved that you were *somebody*. If you were a good athlete, you didn't have to be funny, smart, or wild. You had it made.

When I started high school, I could play sports again. I made the football and baseball teams my sophomore year. Although I was three years behind all my friends, I told myself it didn't matter. I would catch up. I would win. But I never did. An ankle injury put me on the sideline. My injury did not keep me from drinking and carousing. I gave up on athletics.

And I gave in to a lifestyle of drunken recklessness. That's when the Lord saved me, *literally*. It was the fall of my junior year. I started reading then, reading the Bible, C.S. Lewis, everything. And I never stopped. I found out that I could make straight A's when I wanted to. I also found out that there was an advantage to being perceived as smart. And the older you got, the greater the advantage became.

By the time I entered seminary, I had discovered that not only did I have an ability to think theologically, but I also had a facility with languages. Greek, Hebrew, and other languages were easy for me to learn, even fun. In seminary no one knew who had played sports in high school or college, or if they did, they didn't care. Everyone, though, knew who the "A" students were.

The common mantra repeated by faculty and students was that your grades did not reflect your spirituality. I'm not sure anyone really believed it. I didn't. I know for a fact that throughout my whole academic training, I have always been treated differently from those whose grades were lower. Doors were opened for me that were closed for others. After the first year of my doctoral program, I finally made the team. Two of our

Old Testament professors were taking leaves of absence for two years. I was picked to fill in.

"Professor Deere."

That was better than batting cleanup.

I was a professor. And not just any professor, like a professor of English or chemistry. I was a professor of the most important subject of all, theology, the study of God. And not just any branch of theological studies—I was a professor of perhaps the most difficult discipline of all, Old Testament exegesis and Semitic languages. As a result, people all the way from my fellow professors to my peer group to my parishioners treated me with a new level of respect.

Nobody ever told me it was dangerous to be a theological professor, particularly a young one. And no one ever told me that if you tried to find your identity in being smart, especially theologically smart, you would wind up heartsick. No one, that is, until now.

This prophet was amazing. He was right. I was heartsick. I knew it, but I hid it. From everyone.

Joy, pain, confusion, awe. Was there an emotion I hadn't felt yet? Still I would not let the wall come down. For years, I had practiced controlling my emotions, monitoring them ever so carefully. I continued to stare nonchalantly at the Eddie Bauer prophet. All he could read in my face was, *Maybe, maybe not.*

The southern accent, now almost soothing, started again on the same theme.

"All of that frustration was necessary to prepare you to fulfill the call that God has on your life."

So, there *was* a purpose behind the heartsickness. It was the mercy of God inviting me to travel a new road. There was a call on my life, but I had not yet entered into that call. Everything so far was just preparation. God would not let me succeed on an athletic field, but neither would he let me die drunk in a car wreck. He let me succeed in academics, but he would not let me remain intoxicated by that success. He sent my heartsickness to warn me of the danger of building my identity on such shaky foundations as athletics and academics.

I felt relief over my athletic failure. It would never haunt me again. I was never supposed to excel in sports because God had something more excellent for me. Faith and hope danced together joyfully in my heart. Outwardly, though, I sat out the dance, still stoic, still staring.

Next subject.

"You're in a conflict right now, and you think there are only three people on your side. The Lord says to tell you that there are five more on your side."

I *was* in a conflict, and I *did* think only three people stood by me. Besides me, the only one in the room who knew about this was Leesa. There was no way the prophet could know about the conflict. Yet he did. How did he know this? How did he know any of these things?

I was astounded. He was a real prophet. And God was a real God. Of course he is; we all know that. But sometimes he seems so distant and so removed from our troubles. Sometimes it seems that all we have to lead us into battle is a textbook on war, when what we really need is a wise and courageous captain. I heard the voice of my Captain in those prophetic words. He was telling me not to worry, that he would lead me through the minefields of this conflict.

By now, I should have dropped my guard. Instead, I

continued to hold back the tears and look unimpressed by the Lord's loving omniscience.

Next subject.

The future. The prophet left the subject of my past and went to my future. These predictions, I think, were meant for me to ponder, not to publish. Since these words were exclusively about the future, they, of course, could not be verified. But because he had gotten four key facts about my past correct and given them a meaningful interpretation, I believed his predictions.

I should have fallen on my knees like the psalmist, crying out to the nations to give glory to God, but I couldn't. My façade of indifference remained intact. Maybe it was stubbornness. Maybe it was pride. Or maybe it was some sickness in me that rendered a public display of emotion impossible. But maybe I was just making sure of the prophecy by not giving the prophet any last-minute clues. That way, when it was all over, I would know it was all God, and that I had not influenced any of it.

Now the prophet was finished with me.

There was no longer a reason for me to maintain the façade. It was over. The prophet had told me the secrets of my heart. The secret prayer of my ministry. The secret pain of my childhood. The secret frustration of my adolescence. The secret heartsickness of my adulthood. The secret conflict of my present life. With each secret came a promise that gave me freedom from the past and hope for the future. The prophet was real. I wanted to shout for joy to the Lord, but I didn't know how. Instead, I simply said, "Thanks."

"You're welcome," he replied. No one else said a word. The room had been so silent while he was revealing my secrets that I had forgotten anyone else was in the room.

Next he shifted his attention to my wife. He was just as accurate and meaningful with her. Leesa put up no shield. She did not need one. It took only a few sentences before tears streamed down her face and sobs revealed the transparent honesty by which she lived. His soft southern voice continued calmly right through her tears, healing and promising. But that is Leesa's story to tell, not mine.

When we were walking out of the room, Mike asked me, "Was any of that accurate or meaningful to you?"

"All of it was right on the money. Couldn't have been more correct," I said.

"You've got to be kidding. I was watching your face the whole time. I was sure you thought it was all just a bunch of bull!"

"I had been warned."

"Oh, *now* I understand."

I walked out of that drab room into a colorful fall day. I was elated with the discovery that prophets were indeed alive and well. I was in love with prophetic ministry. I was ready to articulate its virtues to anyone who would listen.

I made a more profound discovery that morning, one I could not articulate then. I had worked so hard to overcome the pain of my past, to become somebody special. Others thought I was special, but I felt sick at heart. Then, through the words of the prophet, God's healing love came to me, reinterpreting my past, present, and future. God told the prophet all about my pain because God wanted me to know that he had always been there. Always. Watching over the little boy robbed of his father, watching over the frustrated athlete, watching over the drunken rebel, and watching over the heartsick scholar. Why? Because I *was* special to him. That was my discovery. I had preached that truth to others many times. But you can preach a truth without feeling the truth for yourself. Now I felt that I had always been special to him, and feeling this made me love God all the more. Through the prophet God was removing the burden of trying to be special, and he was telling me that I had never needed to look beyond his love to find my significance. Divine romance had just sneaked back into my life, and its calling card was a happiness that I felt but could not, at that moment, explain.

I was dazed by some of the prophet's words. What did it mean that God would give me new fathers? How would the other promises be fulfilled? Did I have to do anything special? I did not know it then, but now I know that mystery, wonder, and awe had all blissfully returned to my life through that prophetic encounter.

Along with that blissful return came a frightful suspicion—a suspicion that I had crossed some threshold and that my life would never be as predictable or as comfortable as before. After a long, prodigal absence, adventure had finally returned to my life.

Above all, I wondered, *How had this prophet been able to tell me all about my past and my future?* The answer to that question is what this book is all about. Somebody finally told me. Now, I want to tell you.

TWO

Discovering Your Gift

I want to tell you a story, a story about an incredible man. His name is Paul Cain. He was born in 1929, the year the stock market crashed. His family barely survived the Depression. His dad supported a family of five on ten cents an hour doing yard work around the little town of Garland, Texas.

Back then it cost a dime to see a movie. Paul remembers when he was a little boy, trying to watch the picture show, only to have the movie interrupted with a vision of his father. He would see his father bent over a rake in the August sun, the sweat running down his forehead and dropping off the tip of his nose on the lawn of a family better off than his. The vision tormented him. His father had paid for the hour-and a-half movie with an hour of his own sweat.

That was the first hint of young Paul's prophetic calling.

Who could have known then that this little boy from a poor family was about to see the splendor of the Lord and receive a gift that would change lives all over the world?

Paul had just turned eight when he made his faith in Jesus public by walking down the aisle of his Baptist church. Shortly after that, he and his older sister, Mildred, walked to a prayer meeting at the First Assembly of God church nearby. While Paul was kneeling at the altar praying, he felt a presence envelop him. It scared him. He felt that he was either going to die or be taken up into heaven. He got up without finishing his prayers, found his sister, and ran home. But the presence went with him.

In fact, the presence intensified on the way home. He felt an increasing, frightening, inexpressible pleasure. By the time he crawled into bed, he thought the unbearable pleasure would annihilate him. Then the room filled with light brighter than the noontime Texas sun. Out of the light a voice called out, "Paul, Paul."

The terrified little boy shook, shut his eyes, and pulled the covers over his head. The audible voice became a whisper.

"Before you were born, I prepared a special ministry for you."

The light and the presence retreated. The room returned to normal. But not Paul. He would never be normal again. He had been visited by ecstasy and called to be a prophet.

From the first century on, God has visited Christian mystics and lovesick saints, and sometimes even his enemies, in similar fashion. They struggled for words to express the inexpressible pleasure and terror they felt in the presence of pure Happiness and Holiness.

An eight-year-old certainly had neither the words to describe such a visitation nor the frame of reference to understand it. He did not know it then, but that night his prophetic training had begun. And God himself would personally oversee it.

From that night forward, Paul knew things that ordinary people didn't. Sitting around the table at family gatherings, for example, he often knew what his relatives were thinking. At first, he did not recognize his ability to "listen in" on the thoughts of others as anything special, nor did he connect it to his visitation. He assumed everyone could do it. When he innocently began to reveal what he thought everyone else knew, he found out, to his embarrassment, that he had a singular gift. The gift created conflicts as well as confusion. He could not reconcile the pleasant smiles of the relatives he loved with the jealousy and anger they masked.

He frequently saw things that others could not see, things like angels and demons. Sometimes before he walked into a home, he would see who was inside, what they were wearing, and what they were doing. Paul's Southern Baptist pastor, Dr. Parish, recognized that the little boy was special. He used to take Paul with him to visit people in the church, so he could take advantage of the fledgling prophet's knowledge, knowledge he found helpful in ministering to his flock.

Paul's dramatic call, his depth of detailed insight, and the degree of his gifting are unusual, but the way it illustrates God's sovereignty is not. Like most of the prophets in the Bible, Paul never asked for the gift. God just visited him and called him as he did the little boy Samuel (see 1 Sam. 3:1-18). Paul never asked for any supernatural experiences. They just happened. Some of them were so strange that it would take him almost fifty years before he understood their significance. We will return to Paul's story later, but for now let me just point out that God is still using the "ready-or-not-here-I-come" approach with which he surprised Paul.

How Gifts Are Given

Paul Cain's gifting came to him in a sovereign way, unsought and initially misunderstood. This may be the most common way that people receive a prophetic gifting. I am constantly meeting people at conferences who are baffled by sudden and unsought prophetic experiences. "What's happening to me?" they ask. Here is just one example.

Sovereign Impartation

Recently, a lady named Lynette told me a dream that terrified her. She saw a huge pit thirty feet deep filled to the brim with poisonous snakes. Little babies were playing on top of the snakes. Then she heard a voice in the dream say, "Get the babies away from the brood of vipers!"

Lynette wanted to know what the dream meant. She had never heard the phrase "brood of vipers" until the dream. I explained to her that this was Jesus' description of the religious leadership opposing him (see Matt. 12:34; 23:33). Those leaders had a religious poison that so swelled the hearts of its victims that they could not absorb the life of God. In her dream they represented the leadership of some churches today. The babies were new converts or those coming to church for the first time. Instead of being nursed by the milk of God's Word, they were poisoned by the leaders of the church.

She told me she was regularly having vivid dreams like this. They had started recently and without warning. She had not been praying for dreams. Neither had she prayed for impressions about people, which she was now beginning to have. The impressions were not based on her knowledge of people. They seemed to come from nowhere. Sometimes they seemed more like an inner voice than an impression. She wanted to know what was happening to her. She had not sought any of this. In fact, she was a member of a church that vehemently opposed the gifts of the Spirit.

I had some good news and some bad news for Lynette. The good news was she was being called into prophetic ministry. The bad news was she was being called into prophetic ministry.

This meant that one day she would rejoice in revelation, and the next, both she and her friends would question her sanity. And on all days the brood of vipers would have it in for her.

Sometimes prophetic gifts begin like this. The Lord doesn't bother to announce himself. He just turns on the tap of prophetic experiences, interrupting the boredom of an utterly predictable religious life. He is pouring mystery and adventure back into our lives so we may live in that realm where all things have become new (see 2 Cor. 5:17).

The text that describes this sovereign impartation is 1 Corinthians 12:11—"All these [spiritual gifts] are the work of one and the same Spirit, and he gives them to each one, just as he determines."

The Holy Spirit has sovereignly given spiritual gifts to every believer in the body of Christ so that we may better serve one another (see 1 Pet. 4:10). Often these giftings come at the time of conversion. This has led some to conclude that we get all the spiritual gifts we can ever get at that time, and that we have no influence over the Spirit's decisions. Under this view, if you would like to have the gift of prophecy but you did not get it at the time of your conversion, you simply cannot have it, ever.

But Scripture and experience show otherwise.

Apostolic Impartation

The apostle Paul told Timothy "to fan into flame the gift of God, which is in you through the laying on of my hands" (2 Tim. 1:6). The word translated "gift" in this passage refers to spiritual gifts. Paul wrote to the Christians at Rome, "I long to see you so that I may impart to you some spiritual gift to make you strong" (Rom. 1:11). Paul knew that he had the authority to impart spiritual gifts that were not given at the time of someone's conversion.

I do not want to argue about whether we have apostles today, but everyone can acknowledge that we do have leaders who carry more authority than others. They may have apostolic functions. When they are led by the Lord to lay hands on someone and pray for giftings, people can receive spiritual gifts, or their gifts can increase in strength.

John Wimber, who for many years pastored the Vineyard Christian Fellowship of Anaheim, California, and who was the leader of the Vineyard movement, had authority to impart spiritual gifts. Years ago, John brought me before the church one Sunday evening, laid his hands on me, and prayed that the healing and word of knowledge gifts in me would go to a new level. The next day I left on a ministry trip to another country.

In one of those ministry trip meetings, after I had finished the message, I saw a man who appeared to be in his early sixties. I "knew" he feared getting Alzheimer's. I don't know how I knew his fear. I did not have a vision or hear an inner voice, but the second I noticed him, I knew the fear of Alzheimer's tormented him. This kind of thing happened regularly to Wimber, but had never happened to me.

"Sir, do you have a fear of getting Alzheimer's?" I asked.

"Well, I suppose everyone has a fear of getting old," he replied.

"But do you think you are destined for Alzheimer's?"

"Yes. Yes, I do," he finally admitted. It embarrassed him to admit his fear publicly. He had not told anyone about his secret torment. But God knew and stopped the torment that day through a prophetic word and prayer.

This kind of experience happened to me repeatedly on that trip. The impartation I had received from Wimber gave me a new level of revelatory and healing gifts.

Prophetic Impartation

Timothy received another spiritual gift sometime after his conversion. Paul told him, "Do not neglect your gift, which was given you through a prophetic message when the body of elders laid their hands on you" (1 Tim. 4:14). Some of the elders may have been prophets, or they may have laid hands on Timothy in response to a word from one of the prophets in the congregation. I have seen prophetic gifts given or activated in this way many times. I have seen it happen with the laying on of hands and sometimes just through a simple word from a prophet uttered over a believer.

Leesa had a prophetic encounter like this. When I was a theological professor and a complete disbeliever in all contemporary supernatural experience, she had a dream about a couple in our church who were shortly to be married. In the dream the marriage turned out to be made in hell. The husband became abusive, cruel, and unfaithful. "What do you make of that dream?" Leesa asked me.

"Sounds strange to me. Did you have an upset stomach when you went to bed?" Both of us were sure the dream did not come from God. I was sure God was not speaking like that anymore. Leesa thought the dream was not true because we all believed the groom was a great guy. It never occurred to us that her dream was given to keep us from being deceived by appearances. So we forgot the dream and went to the wedding. Later we watched the marriage disintegrate, just as in the dream. But we had forgotten the dream.

Years later, after we had begun to believe in the gifts of the Spirit, we were in an informal meeting with some teachers and prophets. One of the very gifted prophets, John Paul Jackson, prophesied to Leesa that she would have prophetic dreams. The dreams started that night and have continued ever since. In Leesa's case I think she had received a prophetic gifting long before John Paul spoke over her. The dream about the bad marriage, years earlier, was confirmation of this. The prophecy did not bestow her gifting. It simply activated it.

Personal Prayer for Gifts

Some feel that since the Holy Spirit gives gifts "just as he wills," it is useless to pray for gifts. But this is both a misunderstanding of God's sovereignty as well as a misunderstanding of the Scriptures. God is sovereign. He does *everything* just as he wills (see Eph. 1:11). But this does not mean that our actions have no effect on God. We can grieve God (see Eph. 4:30), and we can delight God (see Ps. 147:11). Jesus teaches that our prayers can influence God's activity in this life. He said, "If you believe, you will receive whatever you ask for in prayer" (Matt. 21:22). James put the same principle in negative form, "You do not have, because you do not ask God" (James 4:2). Ultimately, the reconciliation of divine sovereignty and effective human prayers is a mystery. The Scripture teaches both. So pray for the gifts you want, because your prayers may affect the Holy Spirit's desire to give you gifts.

The same apostle who wrote that the Holy Spirit gives gifts "just as he determines" also encouraged his readers to pray for new spiritual gifts for themselves. If someone speaks in tongues, he or she should pray for an interpretation (see 1 Cor. 14:13), which is also a spiritual gift (see 1 Cor. 12:10). God is answering prayers today for spiritual gifts. If you want the gift of prophecy, pray for it. The following section will help you know if you have received a prophetic gift.

Recognizing Prophets

Three revelatory abilities mark the ministry of prophets, although the strength of these abilities will vary from prophet to prophet. First, they can accurately predict the future. Both Joseph and Agabus knew that worldwide famines were coming (see Gen. 41:25-32; Acts 11:27-28). Second, they can reveal to us the present priorities of the Lord for our lives. For example, they may know when we should or should not fast (see Joel 1:14; 2:12, 15; Mark 2:18-20). They may call us to repentance or to a new ministry. They help each of us to find out the various ways in which we may please the Lord in the present moment (see Eph. 5:10). Third, prophets can shed light on the mysteries of our lives or make sense of our pain. For instance, Isaiah knew one of the reasons why righteous people die before their time. God spares them from the trouble to come (see Isa. 57:1). Sometimes prophets can tell us why our religious practices, such as fasting, are ineffective (see Isa. 58:3-6; Jer. 14:12; Zech. 7:4-7). Or as I mentioned in the first chapter of this book, a prophet helped me understand the purposes behind the athletic frustration of my youth and the disenchantment with the academic success of my early career.

In short, prophets tell us the things we cannot see. They do it by revelation from God, not through the study of contemporary trends, philosophy, or psychology. They do it to encourage, comfort, and strengthen us so that we can see and marvel at the beauty, splendor, power, goodness, and wisdom of Jesus. Seeing more of him, we fall more in love with him. That is why God has given us prophets.

Recognizing Your Gift

Any Christian can prophesy occasionally without being a prophet, just as one can lead someone to Christ without being an evangelist. A prophet or prophetess is someone who prophesies consistently and accurately. The occasional experience of a gift may lead us to falsely conclude that it is our main gift, but if we habitually try to minister from the wrong gifting, frustration and failure are inevitable.

This is not a bad thing. For some of us it is necessary to learn how we are *not* gifted before we can discover how we *are*. God will also use the frustration of failure to purify our motives for ministry.

One of the ways we recognize our gifting is that we don't have to work hard to make it happen. Prophets don't have to strive for revelation. It simply comes to them unbidden, and if they wait on the Lord, it will increase. The same is true for evangelists, teachers, administrators, and healers. We do need to strive to acquire godly character, but our gifts, by definition, are *given*.

There are other clues to discovering our gift, but first let's look at a common mistake people make when they try to discover prophetic giftings.

A False Clue

"I'm called as a prophet," the young man told me.

"How do you know?" I asked.

"Because I'm always seeing what is wrong with people, churches, and ministry."

"I'll bet your gifting has brought you a lot of joy."

"No, just the opposite. The people I've ministered to don't really understand the office of prophet. They get offended at the Word of the Lord. What do you think is wrong?"

The young man may have had a prophetic calling, but he had missed the main point of prophetic ministry. He was paying for his misunderstanding with a joyless, strife-filled life. Always seeing what is wrong with people is not a gift; it's an obsession. It is frequently the sign of a rigid, angry, controlling personality disorder that causes pain for everyone involved.

In another church, an angry couple said to me, "We don't understand. We've told those leaders repeatedly what is wrong with their ministry, but they never listen to us. You come here for two days and say the same things, and they listen to *you!*" This couple, oblivious to their bitterness and to their lack of divine authority, had modeled their prophetic ministry after Old Testament prophets, who expressed God's holy anger toward corrupt leaders and a rebellious people.

God is still angry with rebellious leaders (just read Matthew 23). But when he wants to reveal his anger through a human messenger, he normally bestows divine authority on a godly and mature servant, not a beginning prophet.

Faultfinding and anger are not the signs of a prophetic calling, but rather of a wounded heart that has refused God's healing mercy.

The New Testament prophet is called primarily to build up, not to tear down. Anger usually tears down by disheartening people or enflaming them with revenge. Holy anger may frighten rebellious leaders into repentance, but the majority of people to whom New Testament prophets minister will be weak and immature believers, not rebellious people or corrupt leaders. The real prophetic gift is not simply being able to see what's wrong with people but seeing how to build them up.

It does not take much of a gift to make people feel guilty. But imparting grace and mercy requires a highly developed prophetic gift. The gift fills both the hearers and the prophet with divine joy and faith.

After my first encounter with a prophet, I walked out of the room dazzled by the omniscience, wisdom, mercy, goodness, and love of God. I was filled with joy. My faith went off the charts. My passion for the Lord increased. And I wanted to introduce all my friends to prophetic ministry.

How different would it have been if I had faced an angry person who wanted to berate me for my sins? To be sure, I had sins worthy of berating, but God knew that berating me would not lead me to repentance. Instead he fascinated me with his wisdom and dazzled me with his love. That revelatory encounter made sin so uninteresting!

Here are some ways to find out if God is calling you to that kind of ministry.

The Desires of Our Heart

One of the most common ways that God leads us is through our desires. Some Christians believe just the opposite. They think God's will involves going where you do not want to go, doing what you do not want to do, and being what you do not want to be. In short, being miserable. One pretty young woman once told me she feared God was going to make her marry an ugly man or a minister. No offense, she said. I could tell she was debating which alternative would be worse. She was tricked into believing the will of God for her would always be some degree of punishment. Perhaps guilt led her to feel like this. Or maybe someone had taught her that all desires are bad and never to be trusted. She did, in fact, end up marrying a minister.

The Bible has a more positive view of our desires. It holds out the promise, "Delight yourself in the Lord and he will give you the desires of your heart" (Ps. 37:4). If the Lord is our principal source of joy, then we can trust the desires of our heart to lead us.

Do you desire a prophetic gifting? Are you delighting in the Lord? If so, this is a sign he is leading you into a prophetic ministry. Do not be afraid to follow your desires. If his yoke really is easy and his burden really is light, why would he call you to serve him with a gifting that is disagreeable to you?

The Counsel of Others

When I became convinced that the Bible taught the gift of prophecy was for today, I became nervously open to it. But when God came to me through prophecy with his healing love, I wanted the gift of prophecy. Back then, since I did not have much faith in my desires, I needed the advice of some of my trusted friends to obtain the confidence to pursue prophecy for my own ministry. Proverbs affirms that God may use our friends to lead us, "Plans will fail for lack of counsel, but with many advisers they succeed" (Prov. 15:22).

I also received a number of unsolicited and convincing prophetic words from people who did not know me, indicating I should pursue both the prophetic and healing ministries.

Ask those who really know you what they think about your gifting. And don't be afraid to ask prophetic people to pray for you.

Trying It Out

If you regularly have prophetic experiences, this indicates you have a prophetic gifting. In the beginning, this sometimes can be a little frightening. You may know things about others without being told. You may hear a still small voice, or fall into a trance, or, like Ezekiel, be transported to another place in a vision. These experiences may cause you to think you are going crazy. Of course, there's always that possibility, but more likely it is the Lord bringing you a prophetic gift.

Another way you can know if you have a prophetic gifting is by the accuracy of your words when you attempt to minister prophetically and by whether or not they build others up.

In the end, there is no escape from simply trying to move out in the gifting you desire. The best place to try prophetic ministry is *not* in your local church in a Sunday morning service, especially when your church is not enthusiastic about prophets. A better way to explore your gifting is with a few like-minded friends or in a home group committed to training people in the gifts.

Before we proceed, two cautions are in order. First, the group needs to have a leader. Leaderless groups usually go nowhere. Second, the group must be under the authority of your church and have the blessing of the church's leaders. I cannot overstress this. How can we expect God to bless our home group or us if we are not honoring the authority structure of his church? The leader should inform the elders or pastor about the nature, time, and place of the meeting. The meeting should be open to anyone in the church who wants to come. Some churches discourage home groups because they can be misused to foster an elitist mentality—"We are more spiritual than the rest of the church"—and because they can promote critical attitudes and even rebellion to church authority. The group that has a godly leader in submission to the authority of the church's leaders can avoid all of this.

When I lead a home group like this, we spend fifteen or twenty minutes worshipping God. Then I usually teach for fifteen minutes on a theme dealing with equipping for ministry. Next, we ask the Lord to guide us in ministering to one another. Someone might have a vision or an impression. A relevant text of Scripture might come to mind that leads us to pray for a specific person. Often we are led to pray for healing, guidance, the release of gifts, or other practical things relating to ministry. We might have a time of sharing before we end the meeting by praying for the individuals singled out through the prophetic words. Sometimes the most exciting things happen after the meeting is over.

One of the things I love about these kinds of meetings is that I never really know what is going to happen. The kindness and mercy of the Lord continually surprise me.

Because of his kindness and mercy we do not have to worry about discovering our gift. The Giver has promised that those who seek will find their gifts. Our search is really only a response to his pursuit and to his longing for us.

Whether we are eight years old or eighty, and whether in an encounter in a home group, in a meeting with a prophet, or in a luminous, frightening visit in our bedroom, God is pursuing us. He wants to make prophets out of some of us, but ultimately he wants to make friends out of all of us, friends who are fascinated by the mystery and adventure of his holy love.

THREE

Learning How God Reveals

With a whispered secret, the healing began.

She was in her early twenties, with long blond hair and sad eyes. She was also nervous. None of us knew her. It was her first time to visit our church. Standing at the front among a crowd of others who had come forward for prayer, I prayed for God to heal her of a chronic physical ailment. Nothing happened. I prayed again. Still nothing. Nothing appeared to be all she was going to get. Until a young man named Carl whispered her secret.

Carl was a new Christian whom I was training to pray for the sick. He stood beside me, observing my fruitless prayers. Then he whispered to me, "Ask her if she feels like God won't heal her because of the abortion she had when she was eighteen."

I thought, *There is no way I'm going to ask a total stranger such a personal and painful question!*

Then I thought about Carl. He had been a Christian for only six months, but he had been demonstrating a remarkable prophetic gift.

Then I thought about the sad young woman. What did she have to lose if Carl was wrong? What did she have to gain if Carl was right? There was only one way to find out.

"Forgive me if this is off the wall or too invasive," I said to the young woman, "but are you feeling like God won't heal you because of the abortion you had when you were eighteen?"

Her shock told me the answer before she could speak.

The shock gave way to sobs.

There was that reservoir of pain again.

It was not like mine, a reservoir of bitterness and anger because of a wrong done to me. Her unhealed pain came from something she had done wrong. Something she thought could never be made right. Something she thought she would have to live with until the day she died. They told her it was just a choice, her right. But after she chose, she knew it was more than just a choice. Nobody ever told her about the strength of a mother's love, or what happens to a mother when she says no to that love.

Now her heart floated on a reservoir of condemnation. She drank from that reservoir every day of her life. She kept her secret from her friends. But the secret was always there, behind every laugh, spoiling every joy, whispering that she could never be forgiven, never be happy. And whenever she saw a young mother holding a baby...

Because she could not bring herself to tell her secret to anyone, nobody ever told her that God longed to forgive her and set her free. Nobody ever told her that God thought about her every single day, longing to woo her with his love. Nobody ever told her. The secret stood in the way. It kept the dam of the reservoir intact.

God had decided it was time to break the dam. So, he gave her secret to a newborn Christian, a baby prophet.

"How did you know? How did you know?" she sobbed, her head still down, eyes still closed.

"God told us."

When she opened her eyes, she searched our expressions. She knew we were God's representatives, and now we knew her secret. She expected to see condemnation. Instead she saw two men enraptured with God's all-knowing love. Now it was her turn to be enraptured by the splendor of that love.

When she heard that God longed for her, that he was ready to forgive her right then, that he was ready to make her laugh again, and that Jesus had died for her to make all this possible, the dam broke and the condemnation came flooding out of her.

She walked out of the church hopeful and happy, loved and forgiven.

And it all happened through a revelation.

The Meaning of Revelation

Revelation is God making known to us what we did not know or could not have known through our natural senses.

How did Carl know about the abortion? In his mind's eye he saw a woman dressed in a long gown, standing on the young woman's shoulder and whispering in her ear that she could not be healed because of the abortion at age eighteen. Yes, I know that sounds weird. And no, I don't have a biblical text for it.

I don't even have an exact interpretation of what Carl saw. Was it a vision in which the miniature gowned lady represented the young woman's conscience? Did he see a spiritual reality, a demonic accuser assigned to torment her? Who knows? God knew, but he did not care to tell us any more about the vision. Revelation is often like that, answering a critical question you did not even know to ask, and in the answering, raising new questions left unanswered. All of us who want to follow God, especially prophets, have to get used to walking in unexplained realms.

For whatever reason, God has chosen to vary the clarity, intensity, and means of his revelation. This can make revelation difficult to understand. It can also affect our certainty over whether or not it is really God speaking. Consider the following examples.

When a biblical prophet said, "God spoke to me," he usually meant that the message from God was not mixed with the prophet's opinion or interpretation. He was certain he was speaking the words of God and nothing else. If the prophet said, "The hand of the Lord was upon me," he meant that the divine message was coming with greater power than usual (see Ezek. 3:22). And if he said, "The Lord spoke to me with his *strong hand* upon me," he meant the message was impressed deep into his soul with compelling power (see Isa. 8:11). But not all revelation comes with this force.

Sometimes the apostles did not have the certainty of "God said." Instead, they had to be content with, "It seemed good to the Holy Spirit and to us..." (Acts 15:28). On other occasions they had even less clarity or certainty. The instantaneous healing of a lame man at Lystra rested on something as flimsy as an impression (see Acts 14:9-10).

The prophet who is always careful to indicate the level of certainty of his message is not only wise but also mature.

The Bible's authors did not always explain the words they used when they wrote about their prophetic experiences. This also complicates studying revelation. For example, Paul never tells us the difference between a "word of knowledge," a "revelation," a "prophecy." The phrase "word of knowledge" is used only one time and in a context that does not allow us to define it with certainty.

This means we will learn more about revelation by paying greater attention to concrete examples of how God spoke to the prophets rather than by trying to define revelatory terms. So, how *did* God speak to the prophets?

The Means of Revelation

The primary way that God speaks to all believers is through the written word of God, the Bible. The Bible has more authority than present-day, personal revelation because its authority extends to all people everywhere and at all times. (I discuss reasons for the unique authority of the Bible at length in *Surprised by the Voice of God*, pp. 278-80.) Prophets are obligated to study and meditate on the Scriptures just as much as teachers and other believers are. However, in addition to the Bible, prophets will regularly hear the voice of God through other means.

Appearances of the Lord

We read that no one can see God and live (see Ex. 33:20). And yet he appeared to his friends and even to an occasional enemy (see Gen. 20:3). Sometimes he appeared in a dream or a vision. Other times he appeared in a physical form (see Gen. 18:1ff). Sometimes he came as the angel of the Lord (see Ex. 3:2ff). Other times he came wrapped in his glory (see Ex. 16:10; 33:18–34:8). He appeared to help at moments of crisis, at turning points in the history of his people, at moments of rebellion to warn or to judge, and sometimes he appeared simply to share his plans or to promise a blessing. If no one can see God, whom were they seeing when he appeared?

It must have been the Son of God (see John 1:14-18).

One of the striking things about these appearances is that they were not really necessary. If the Father's purpose was simply to supply us with some information, he could have sent angels in the place of his Son. But God wanted to send his best. And the Son *wanted* to come.

When you are in love, you long to be with the one you love. You are not content simply to send messengers and write letters to your beloved. You want to go yourself. You want to charm that beautiful person. You want to make your lover's eyes sparkle. Look behind these appearances to his people, and you will see the heart of God burning with passion. Indeed, the energy propelling all forms of revelation is God's incomparable, radiant, holy love for us.

God loves us and wants to be with us. This is the greatest mystery I know. And the longer I ponder this mystery, the greater it grows.

One last point. If in the past God appeared in his glory to a grumbling, ungrateful people (see Ex. 16:9-10), why wouldn't he appear today to a people seeking him with all their hearts?

Angels

Angels are "ministering spirits sent to serve those who will inherit salvation" (Heb. 1:14). Angels do many things for us. They protect us when we walk through fire, deliver us from the hand of the enemy, and bring messages to us from heaven. When we leave this life, they escort us to heaven (see Luke 16:22). Angels may appear in their glory or in human form as a guest in our home without ever revealing their real identity (see Heb. 13:2). Or they may perform their service for us, giving us no hint of their presence. Yet prophets often see them when others cannot (see 2 Kings 6:15-17).

Recently, a godly prophetess that I have known for years told me the following story, which I believe. Lying sick on her bed in the afternoon, discouraged by what she perceived as a lack of spiritual progress, this woman cried out to God to change her. Although her eyes were closed, and although she never heard the bedroom door open, she knew someone had just entered the room. Someone was coming toward the bed. She was afraid to open her eyes. Now someone was hovering over her. Then she felt the softest, gentlest hands on her face, first laid together vertically covering her cheeks and eyes, then removed, and then one hand laid horizontally across her forehead. This was repeated three times.

She opened her eyes.

Standing beside her bed was an elderly lady five feet tall. She wore a royal blue dress, and her hair was covered with a royal blue sash.

"Thank you," said the prophetess.

"If you are interested in changing, now is the time," said the lady, who then turned her head to look through the window beside the bed.

"I have to go now," she said as she floated upward through the ceiling.

This was not a vision. It was a visitation. The prophetess was wide awake during the whole experience, which lasted about a minute, and she felt immediate spiritual and physical effects after this encounter.

The next morning the prophetess bounded out of bed at sunrise, filled with energy. The headache, sore throat, and tiredness that had harassed her for a week were gone. She was happy. She felt so special to God. He had sent an angel to touch her. Now she was confident that she could change and would change.

I believe the angel's message was not just for the prophetess but also for all of us who want to change. Now is the time to change, to prepare for an outpouring of the Holy Spirit. In the Bible, encounters with angels increase just before turning points in the history of God's people. And maybe, just maybe, a turning point in your history lies just around the corner, either through a touch by an angel or through the audible voice of God.

Audible Voice

God spoke in an audible voice to individuals, to crowds, and even to a whole nation. Moses regularly heard the audible voice of the Lord, but outside his experience, the audible voice is the rarest way in the Bible that God speaks (see Num. 12: 6-8). In Scripture the audible voice comes at moments of crisis (see Gen. 22:11-12), or at great turning points such as the giving of the Law at Sinai, the baptism and transfiguration of Jesus, the week before his cross, and the conversion of the apostle Paul.

All of us would like to have the clarity of an audible voice to guide us. But there is a price for that clarity. As a general rule, the clearer the revelation, the more difficult it will be to fulfill the revelation (see *Surprised by the Voice of God,* pp. 131–33). The original clarity and power of the revelation are meant to keep us from giving in to debilitating doubts in the midst of the trial that usually follows the revelation.

God still speaks in an audible voice. Nothing in the Scripture teaches that once the Bible was completed, God would stop speaking in an audible voice. Trusted national, evangelical leaders from our own times report having heard the audible voice of the Lord, and their integrity is without question.

You might think God only speaks in an audible voice to important church leaders. But that is not the case. Though I have never heard the audible voice, I know credible people who have, and some of them are not leaders in the church.

Audible Only to Your Ears

You may hear the voice with your ears, but no one else does, even though someone might be standing beside you when the voice speaks. Samuel heard his name being called so loudly that he thought it must be Eli in the next room. He got out of bed and went to Eli, but Eli denied calling him. This happened two more times before Eli realized that the Lord was speaking audibly to little Samuel, but not to him. Eli told Samuel what he was to say the next time the voice called him, "Speak, Lord, for your servant is listening." Samuel did as he was told, and the Lord gave him his first prophecy (see 1 Sam. 3:1-14).

The Internal, Audible Voice

This is just as clear as the audible voice, only you do not hear it with your ears but in your mind. In the Scripture, the phrase "The word of the Lord came to me saying," probably refers to the internal, audible voice. When some of the elders sat down before Ezekiel, "the word of the Lord came" to Ezekiel, giving him a message for the elders (see Ezek. 14:1ff). It does not appear that Ezekiel was hearing an audible voice.

I have experienced this form of the voice a number of times, but it is the least common way that God speaks to me. And it always involves something that is very important to me.

Sentence Fragments

Maher-Shalal-Hash-Baz. What in the world does *that* mean? Isaiah didn't know either. He was just told to write it down on a scroll (see Isa. 8:1). These are four Hebrew words strung together in an ungrammatical sentence fragment. The words were just as clear as an audible voice, but their meaning was not. They contained a mystery. Sometimes God may speak only a single word. And while the word may be clear, its interpretation may not be. Why would God grant a clear revelation and then hide the interpretation?

He does so for his own glory. Our glory is to search out the meaning (see Prov. 25:2).

The most profound and beautiful truths are simple and clear on the surface. Sadly, that's where most of us stay, on the surface. But when we leave the realm of superficial acceptance of a particular truth and surrender our heart to prolonged contemplation of that truth, we journey into endless realms of mystery.

Consider for a moment the simple truth that God loves us. All of us believe it, but many of us get over it within a few months of our conversion. What would happen to you and to me if we plunged beneath the surface of this fundamental truth? What if we just asked one simple question, "Why would God love us?" And what if we refused to give up the search until we got the answer?

To answer that question we would have to think about God. But in order to think accurately about him, we would have to come into his presence. Once there, we would begin to see him, his beauty, his splendor, and his holiness; the mystery of his love would only increase with each new revelation of his Being. Why would someone like God love people like us? But as the mystery would increase, so would our fascination with the beauty of his holiness. The more we would see, the more we would love. The more we love God for his own sake, the greater the glory we give him. And the greater our glory, for in loving him, we come to resemble him more closely and to reflect more of his glory.

Every revelation to us from an infinite Person can never be more than a partial unveiling of the One who is drawing us after him into eternal realms of mysterious beauty.

That single word from God that defies immediate understanding may have been sent to bring romance, mystery, and glory back into our relationship with him.

A Knowing

There are times when a divine revelation does not come in the form of a voice or spoken message. It may be something you simply know. And there may be no rational reason for *how* you know. When Jesus was talking to the woman at the well, he knew she had had five husbands and was not married to the man with whom she was living (see John 4:18). On other occasions, the Bible simply says Jesus knew someone's thoughts or plans (see Matt. 22:18; Mark 2:8; John 6:15).

After a church service, I frequently wait at the front of the auditorium with a ministry team to pray for people. Often I will know secrets about those coming for prayer. For example, at the end of one service, the pastor invited anyone who had chronic pain to come for prayer. A lady whom I had never met walked toward me. Although I didn't know her, I knew she did not drink. I also knew she was certain she would end up an alcoholic. She had come to the front to get relief from chronic pain, not chronic fears. But her fear was on God's agenda for that day. When I asked her, she admitted that although she did not drink, she was certain she was destined for alcoholism. Satan often torments people with these kinds of fears. That day, the prison of her fears was opened, and the lady was set free.

This is not only a very normal experience for me but for many others. We believe that Jesus is the knower of hearts who reveals the secrets of our hearts to set us free from self-deceptions as well as satanic ones.

Impressions

Impressions differ from inner knowings in that they are less certain. They are a feeling that we ought to do something or that something is true. God uses impressions or feelings to guide us. Nehemiah said, "So my God put it into my heart to assemble the nobles ..." (Neh. 7:5). From a biblical perspective, the heart is the center of the emotions and affections. Nehemiah followed a feeling in his heart, not an audible voice or a prophetic word. He assumed that this feeling came from God. When Paul was preaching at Lystra, he "saw" that a lame man in the audience had the faith to be healed (see Acts 14:9). You cannot physically see faith in or on someone. Paul had a perception, intuition, impression, or feeling that this was true of the man. And when Paul acted on that feeling, the man was healed.

Dreams, Visions, and Trances

God uses dreams to speak to us in our sleep when our defenses are down and we are more receptive. Visions are similar to dreams, but normally they occur while we are awake. Sometimes the Bible makes no distinctions between dreams and visions, using both terms to describe the same experience (see Dan. 7:1-2). A trance is a vision in which we lose the use of our physical senses. Both Peter and Paul fell into trances (see Acts 10:10; 22:17). Although the Old Testament does not use the word trance, it appears that Balaam, Saul, and Daniel all experienced them (see Num. 24:4; 1 Sam. 19:23-24; Dan. 10:9).

Trances are not common in the biblical record, but dreams and visions are:

For God does speak—now one way, now another—though man may not perceive it. In a dream, in a vision of the night, when deep sleep falls on men as they slumber in their beds, he may speak in their ears and terrify them with warnings, to turn man from wrongdoing and keep him from pride, to preserve his soul from the pit, his life from perishing by the sword.   JOB 33:14-18

This applies to the New Testament also, where dreams and visions occur throughout. The last book of the New Testament, for example, is an extended prophetic vision.

Although God speaks to many people in dreams and visions, he does so even more to his prophets (see Num. 12:6). The Bible encourages us to expect a sharp increase in God's use of these visionary experiences:

"In the last days," God says, "I will pour out my Spirit on all people. Your sons and daughters will prophesy, your young men will see visions, your old men will dream dreams. Even on my servants, both men and women, I will pour out my Spirit in those days, and they will prophesy."

ACTS 2:17-18

According to the Bible, dreams and visions are supposed to be a normal part of church life.

Some prophetic dreams and visions may be simple and easy to understand. Others are complex and filled with symbolism. God may use a vision to take a prophet somewhere. Isaiah was taken up to heaven for his commissioning (see Isa. 6:1ff). John was taken to heaven and shown the last days (Revelation).

These experiences are so real that the prophet may not know if he is in his body or in a vision. When Paul was caught up into the third heaven, he could not tell if his journey was physical or spiritual (see 2 Cor. 12:3). Ezekiel was "lifted up by the Spirit" and transported to places where he could see secret sins (see Ezek. 8:3ff). I know a number of prophets today who have had similar experiences, and some who have them regularly.

Why does God speak to his people, especially to his prophets, in visionary language? Why not just sit them down in a comfortable chair with a cup of coffee and put the message into their minds?

Because there is more to us than just a mind. We are also spirit and flesh. And we have emotions that powerfully affect our behavior. Sometimes a picture *is* worth a thousand words. Where we might ignore a worn-out warning, a graphic dream can shake us out of a complacent state. Or a vision of future joy may cause us to endure a present hardship long after we would have forgotten a prosaic promise.

We also live in a world that is filled with mystery and with other spiritual beings very different from us. And although we are created in God's image, bearing a certain similarity to him, he is infinitely more dissimilar (see Isa. 55:8-9). There are realms of truth and experience that transcend human understanding. God's mysterious visitations and visions allow us to experience these realms.

The Natural World

God speaks to us through his creation in at least three different ways. First, the design and beauty of creation reveals the existence of a Designer who is both beautiful and powerful (see Rom. 1:19-20). Second, the natural world bursts with analogies to the spiritual world, which illustrate spiritual principles for us. For example, a lazy person may learn a great deal from observing the ways of the lowly ant (see Prov. 6:6-11). Third, God may illumine natural events to communicate his plans or express his ways. For example, the Lord used a locust invasion to give Joel a message for his nation (see Joel 2:25-27). He used fire, wind, and an earthquake to get his point across to Elijah (see 1 Kings 19:11-12). Jesus used stories about everyday life to reveal divine truth. God will illumine anything in the natural world to speak to us if we have trained our eyes to see, our ears to hear, and our hearts to receive.

Fleeces

God sometimes speaks through "fleeces" (see Judg. 6:36-40). I think it can be appropriate to lay out a fleece when we have to make a decision, especially when we have come to an impasse. We have prayed and waited, but we are still uncertain.

I have three cautions regarding this method of proving God's will. First, make sure the fleece is supernatural and cannot be manipulated by anyone concerned in the decision. Second, use fleeces sparingly and as a last resort. Excessive use of fleeces indicates a view of God that makes him more like a personal genie than a sovereign, almighty God. If we succumb to that view of God, it will lead to a loss of intimacy with him. Third, remember that fleeces are a lower, less personal form of revelation. When we use a fleece, we are confessing either that God has not spoken to us, or that we could not hear him with our hearts, or that what he did say to us has not given us the confidence to act.

Physical Manifestations in Our Bodies

A sick lady touched the hem of Jesus' robe, but Jesus did not feel the touch. Instead he felt healing power leave his body and go into the lady. He felt the sensation, so he stopped to search for the lady because he wanted her to know that it was her faith in him, not the power of his robe, that saved her (see Luke 8:45-46).

Today it is not uncommon for God to speak to prophetic people through bodily signs. One prophet I know feels a physical chill on his body when he is in the presence of an AIDS victim. Sometimes when I am speaking to a group, I feel a pain that is not mine. This helps me to identify people that the Lord may want to heal. As soon as I ask people with the pain to come for prayer, the pain I feel leaves.

Physical manifestations have always been a controversial topic in the church. They are subject to abuse and fabrication. People who have them may feel superior to others. People who do not experience them may think those who do are unstable. But these are not good reasons for rejecting the signs. Any good thing may be abused or counterfeited.

Remember, we are more than our minds. Our bodies are constantly telling us things: when to rest, when to eat, when to see a doctor, and so on. We regularly use our bodies rather than words to communicate love, dislike, apathy, and many other things to one another. If that's the case, why should we think it so strange if God uses our bodies to communicate with us?

If you get physical signs in your body, learn what they mean, don't abuse them, and don't make a big deal out of them.

The Five Spiritual Senses

Bible believers have no difficulty believing that the biblical prophets could see things with their spiritual eyes and hear things with their spiritual ears. Visions are not seen with the natural eyes, and the internal audible voice is not heard with natural ears. But what about the senses of taste, touch, and smell? Do they have spiritual correspondences as well? Even though there is not much biblical evidence for spiritual taste, touch, and smell, there are three lines of evidence arguing that God speaks through these senses as well. First, by analogy we should expect him to do so. Since he speaks to us by spiritual seeing and hearing, we should expect him to transform the other three senses as well unless there is a convincing reason why he wouldn't.

Second, beginning prophets as well as mature prophets are getting messages today through the spiritual senses of taste, touch, and smell. One lady I know frequently "smells" incest victims. When a victim of abuse walks by her at church or a party, she often smells something like sulfur. She then prays for an appropriate time to minister to the wounded one. Third, the devil can use all five senses, too. I have been in the presence of demonic touch, smell, and taste on a number of occasions when we have been casting demons out of people. The devil is not a creator, but a copier and counterfeiter of the works and methods of God. The copy or counterfeit assumes the existence of the real. (Later we will discuss how to protect ourselves from counterfeit revelation.)

A Word of Caution

Prophetic experience is one of the most supernatural experiences in the Bible. It remains so today. There are two common mistakes made by those pursuing supernatural ministry. The first mistake is to think if an angel could just visit us, or if we could just hear the audible voice of God, or be caught up into heaven, all our problems would be solved and we would always have the faith to obey God. But this is not the case.

A whole nation watched as God sent ten plagues on their oppressors. That same nation walked through a sea that God had parted for them. They saw him come down on a mountain in fiery glory and heard him speak to them in an audible voice. And yet, these same people worshipped a golden calf and indulged in sexual orgies.

There were even great prophets who experienced the miraculous power of God but who afterward had significant failures in their lives. Moses had parted the Red Sea and talked with God face to face, and yet at the end of his life he disobeyed God and died outside the Promised Land. Elijah called fire down from heaven and the next minute was running for his life from Jezebel. There is no spiritual experience that will eliminate our need to walk by faith every single day.

The second mistake is to become more enamored with supernatural experience than with the Lord himself. This error is especially common when we are first being introduced to prophetic ministry. If revelation and power become more important to us than friendship with Jesus, we will become poor stewards of the gift entrusted to us, eventually deceiving ourselves and those who follow us.

Since it is the Father's holy love that lies behind all revelation, sending it, protecting it, and interpreting it, we *must* become immersed in that love. For God will trust his secrets and the secrets of others to those who love him and all that he has created.

FOUR

Discerning God's Voice

W hen Mike Bickle told me that one of the most awesome prophets in America lived in Garland, Texas, and that he was willing to meet with me in Dallas, I don't know what I expected. He looked more like a kind grandfather than an awesome prophet, sitting there at the restaurant table with me and three other preachers my age. He was fifty-eight but could have easily passed for sixty-five with his white hair and deep wrinkles. We could have passed for his sons, except he did not have any sons and never would.

He sounded more like a historian than an awesome prophet. He enthralled us with incredible stories of God's power from the healing revival of the early 1950s. He knew all the famous names associated with that movement. He had stood with many of them on stages around the world, and he knew the good and the bad about those people.

He never referred to himself as a prophet. If he made any reference to his revelatory gift, it was from the past. Even then he was very low-key about it. But we weren't really interested in the past. We wanted power for the present, where it would do somebody some good. We had come to learn about revelation from an awesome prophet. We wanted to know the secrets of hearing God's voice. Without being impolite by saying it, we all concluded that this was not the man to teach us about God'svoice. Although he might have been a powerful prophet in his prime, he was definitely past his prime.

None of us were impressed enough even to invite him to our churches to minister. What I was impressed with, though, was his kindness. Even when he was talking about the failures of his contemporaries, his voice was filled with love for them. There was not an ounce of condemnation in the man. But we weren't looking for nice people. We were looking for powerful people, people who could impart that power to us so we, in turn, could impart it to our churches.

I did overlook one thing. His eyes had that otherworldly look, a look I had seen before. But I dismissed them because they did not go with the rest of the package, which was decidedly *un*prophetic.

I did not know those eyes were gazing effortlessly into the souls of four preachers sitting there at the table. I did not know he already knew that one of us had years of suffering ahead, that one of us would fall into sin and leave the ministry, and that one of us would become a son to him. I did not know because he did not tell me. At least, not then.

I also did not know this was a sovereign meeting, arranged long ago by God for my benefit. I did not know it was a test revealing how little discernment I possessed. And I did not know God was teaching me in that very meeting the key to hearing his voice. The sum total of what I did not know would have been overwhelming, had it been possible to overwhelm the mercy of God.

That was my first meeting with Paul Cain, one of the spiritual fathers that God had promised me through another prophet three weeks earlier. However, I failed to recognize him both as a prophet and as a father. I didn't have ears to hear.

Four Tests

God is not the only one who speaks to us. Our own thoughts and emotions speak to us. The pressure we feel from others speaks to us as well. The devil also speaks to us (see Rev. 12:10). All these voices.

How can we discern when it is really God who is the one speaking? Before my introduction to Paul, I would have put almost exclusive emphasis on the following tests to help us distinguish the voice of God from other voices.

The Bible

The world is going to end. Everyone knows that. But *when* it will is the subject of no little theological and scientific debate. Someone, using mathematical calculations based on the Bible, predicted the rapture would occur in September 1988. He acquired a significant number of followers in spite of the fact that Jesus said, "No one knows about that day or hour, not even the angels in heaven, nor the Son, but only the Father" (Matt. 24:36).

The coming of the year 2000 and Y2K fears also led some to predict an exact date for the second coming. One well-known teacher used the numerical values of Hebrew letters in combination with the fact that many older computer programs used 9999 as an exit command, to suggest that the rapture would occur on September 9, 1999 (9-9-99). In his article he even quoted Matthew 24:36, reminding his readers that no one really knew the date of the rapture. However, his article was clearly speculating that it was coming on September 9, 1999.

Speculating about the timing of an event that has been

declared unknowable by an Omniscient Being has never been a very productive use of time. But by paying closer attention to what the Bible has to say, many people have been saved from more than merely wasting time.

When the apostle Paul came to Berea preaching Christ in the Jewish synagogue, for example, the Bereans "examined the Scriptures every day to see if what Paul said was true" (Acts 17:11). Their willingness to scrutinize the Scriptures saved their lives, forever. We too are to follow the example of the noble Bereans. The Bible is the first test through which our subjective experience must pass. If my impression contradicts the Bible, then I discard it. You would think that Bible believers would never accept something as true if it contradicts the Bible, but they do it all the time.

For example, young Christians marry unbelievers all the time, convinced that God has given his blessing, even though the Bible says not to do it (see 2 Cor. 6:14). If we want something badly enough, we can always find a reason why we are an exception to the rule.

Yet Jesus said, "The Scripture cannot be broken" (John 10:35). To my knowledge there are no clear instances of God's breaking his word. He does not tell us to do what the Bible forbids. God's command to Abraham to sacrifice Isaac is sometimes cited as an exception to this principle, but careful study shows it is not (see *Surprised by the Voice of God*, p. 374, note 1). Although the voice of God may contradict one of our interpretations of Scripture, it will never contradict the Bible, no matter what our hearts tell us.

Its Character

For twelve years she woke up every day thinking that she was supposed to die that day. It never occurred to her that the voice telling her this was the voice of a consummate liar.

I met her at a conference in another country. While I was speaking, I had an impression that certain individuals in the audience felt they were going to die before their time. I asked if those who felt that way would come to the front so we could pray for them. Two ladies came forward.

I walked over to one of them. She had red hair and was in her mid-thirties. She looked as if she should be enjoying life, but instead was just enduring it.

"Do you think you are going to die prematurely?" I asked her.

"Yes. That is what I think God is telling me."

"Do you think your children are going to die before their time, too?"

"Yes," she said as she burst into sobs.

"That's not God speaking to you," I told her.

"How do you know?"

"How does the voice make you feel?"

"Hopeless."

"That's why it can't be God. His words bring hope, not despair. How long has the voice been telling you that you and your children are going to die soon?"

"Twelve years."

"That's another reason we know the voice is lying. Twelve years is not soon."

I believe the lady was set free from the tormenting voice that night. The voice threatening a premature death is a common trap. Christians fall into it all the time because we have not learned to recognize the character of the Lord's voice. It isn't as though he never tells people they are close to death. He told the apostle Paul the time for his departure had come (see 2 Tim. 4:6). But the words produced joy and peace in him, not hopelessness and terror. God reserves his terrifying words for those in rebellion against him. He speaks encouraging words to his weak and immature children who may be stumbling, but who are stumbling toward him.

If we read the Bible with the illumination of the Holy Spirit, we will learn to recognize the character of the Lord's voice. In the Scripture we see that when Jesus speaks to his followers, he does not condemn, nag, or whine. His voice is calm, quiet, and authoritative. Even his warnings and rebukes bring hope. If it is really the wisdom of the Lord that is coming to us, it should bring peace if we truly listen (see James 3:17; Phil. 4:6-7; John 16:33).

The voice of the devil does just the opposite. He accuses and condemns us in order to steal our hope and faith (Rev. 12:10).

Voices have different characters. Learn the character of each voice that speaks to you before you attribute it to God.

Its Fruit

What kind of fruit does the inner voice produce when you follow it? Jesus said that we could tell the difference between false and true prophets by the fruit of their ministries (see Matt. 7:15-23). In the same way, if we are following the voice of the Lord, we will see the fruit of the Spirit in our own lives, even if people reject our ministry.

Pay attention to the results of the different voices that you follow. Keep records. What happens when you follow the voice of anger, the voice that says, *God will judge your opponent?* What happens when you follow the voice of greed, the voice that says, *You have to have it now?* What happens when you follow the voice of fear, the voice that says, *You just can't?*

If we are following the voice of God, we can expect to experience the fruit of the Spirit, especially peace (see Phil. 4:9).

Its Content

There are two verses in the Bible that are disbelieved, by Bible believers in every age. Those who fail to believe these verses will also fail to hear much of what God is saying to them. I am referring to Isaiah 55:8-9: "'For my thoughts are not your thoughts, neither are your ways my ways,' declares the Lord. 'As the heavens are higher than the earth, so are my ways higher than your ways and my thoughts than your thoughts.'"

Most of us Christians would say we believe this, but the truth is we believe it for someone else. We tend to think it is the other person who does not understand God's ways.

If God's thoughts and acts differ enormously from ours, two indisputable facts follow. First, the most important things in life can only be understood by divine revelation. The unaided human intellect, no matter how brilliant, will not be able to penetrate the ways of God. Second, when the divine revelation comes, it may seem wrong to us initially.

When Jesus told the disciples that he would be crucified and raised three days later, Peter said, "Never, Lord!" Peter was saying that this was a bad plan. It was the opposite of what should happen. No matter how many times Jesus told the disciples about the cross, they could not understand or accept it. If his best friends could not understand his cross, what about the rest of the world?

The Greeks and Romans thought the message about the cross was utter nonsense. Crucifixion was reserved for the lowest criminal. It was illegal to crucify a Roman citizen no matter what his crime. There was no example either in Greek or in Roman mythology of a crucified god. A crucified god was a contradiction in terms. What god would ever submit to such humiliation? The Jews could not accept the message of the cross, because one who hung on a cross was cursed according to Deuteronomy 21:22-23. They thought it was impossible for God to bring himself under a curse.

The cross of Jesus contradicted human wisdom and experience, and even the scholars' understanding of the Bible. After two thousand years, the cross is still a mystery that is only partially understood. It is normal for God to come to us in a form that makes it difficult to recognize him, and in a way that makes it easy to reject him. How could it be otherwise when we are relating to our Creator, who is infinitely superior to us in every way?

Our inability to recognize him and his ways is one of the reasons he sends us prophets. If we want to be prophets, we have to pay close attention to the thoughts that come to us out of nowhere with a message that contradicts our normal ways of thinking or acting.

These four tests of the voice—Scripture, its character, its fruit, and its content—help us to recognize God's voice. But perhaps you've already noticed these tests have a fatal flaw. That flaw lies in the human heart that tries to use these tests for its own benefit.

I knew these four tests when I first met Paul Cain. In fact, I was even applying them at our lunch meeting. Even so, I still missed what God was saying to me. I thought I was just passing an afternoon with a kind old man whose ministry was over. Instead, God was giving me a deep friendship with a gifted prophet who would help me more than any other person to hear the voice of God. He was giving me more than a friend. He was giving me a father who would prove to be an incredible blessing not only to me, but to my wife and children, and to many, many of my friends in the years following that lunch. But on that day I failed to recognize the prophet, the friend, the father, and the blessing he would be to me. Why? Because I could not see past the packaging to the wonderful gift inside.

It would take almost a year before I began to realize only a little of what the Lord was giving to me in my friendship with Paul. On the other hand, before he left the lunch table, Paul knew that the Lord was binding us together in a special relationship. He also knew that I was oblivious to this fact, and that it would take some time before I caught on. And he knew the cause of my oblivion. Why did he know so much and I so little? The friendship would come in a year, but the answer to that question would not come for several years.

It came on a beach in Perth, Australia.

Embracing Our Weakness

No matter how I looked at it, the night before was an utter failure. How could Paul have bungled it so badly? What was he thinking? Or was it our fault for putting him on that stage on the wrong night? Or was God behind the whole fiasco? To my mind that was the least likely possibility.

In the year following that lunch meeting, Paul and I had more lunches. The lunches turned into regular dinners at our house. We became good friends. My whole family loved Paul. I still had not seen him minister prophetically, so I continued to think of him as more or less past his prime. Then he invited me to join him for two days of ministry at a church in St. Louis. I watched him call out people from the audience and tell them the secrets of their hearts and God's plans for them. He told people their diseases and prayed for them, sometimes pronouncing them healed. I was stunned. I had never seen anything like it. After the meeting, I said, "Paul, why didn't you tell me you could do that?"

"Do what?"

"Do what! Do ministry like that. Call so many people out, knowing all those detailed things about them."

"Oh, I thought I'd told you that the Lord uses me prophetically."

"You did, I guess. But the way you told me made me think your prophetic ministry was all in the past."

From that time on, Paul and I began to minister together. I introduced him to John Wimber, the leader of the Vineyard movement, and the two of them became good friends. Now all three of us were ministering together. And that is what led to the fiasco.

People had come from all over western Australia to the coastal city of Perth in March 1990, to experience Paul's prophetic gift. Many had driven long distances, anticipating miracles and supernatural revelation at the conference John Wimber was hosting.

On the second night of the conference, Paul gave one of his

least helpful messages. He was distracted and had difficulty keeping his thoughts together, even though he was speaking from typewritten notes. Not to worry, because most of the people had not come to hear him teach but to hear him prophesy. After the meandering message, the audience held its breath, waiting for the prophet to call out the secrets of their hearts and tell them the future. It never happened. Paul simply walked off the stage, leaving us to handle the disappointment.

The next day, Paul and I were walking along the beach when I said, "Paul, I have noticed a pattern with you. Sometimes when you teach, it's wonderful, and then you prophesy and it's even better. Other times when you teach, you have difficulty just getting the words out. But that's OK because then you deliver prophetic words that astound us. However, last night neither the teaching nor the prophecy part came off very well. And so many people left disappointed. Why is that?"

"I know what you're asking, Jack," said Paul with one of his grandfatherly smiles. "I know they came to see my gift. And I know I have a wonderful gift. It would be false humility if I said otherwise. But it's a gift, not a talent. The way the Lord made me keeps me from doing anything special with that gift unless he anoints me. I'm not a gold or silver vessel. I'm an unremarkable earthen vessel that contains a remarkable prophetic gift. The Lord put the gift in a plain vessel so the people would never confuse the two, never be tempted to give the glory to me instead of to God. From time to time the Lord reminds the people of my earthen character. Last night he chose not to anoint me, but to display me in my humanity. What I really am, Jack, is a silly old man with a miraculous gift. Last night the Lord decided that the people needed to see just the silly old man without the gift. I don't know why he did that, but I know if I don't accept it, he'll stop using me. The price I pay for my gift is living with the disappointment of people and enduring the embarrassment of being deserted by the anointing."

Until that moment I had never seen someone embrace his thorn in the flesh so humbly and wholeheartedly. It gave me a better understanding of why Paul could be trusted with a powerful gifting and why he is so good at interpreting the prophetic language of the Holy Spirit.

The Humble Heart

Paul Cain had learned the same secret as the apostle Paul—the power of Christ rests on the people who embrace their weaknesses (see 2 Cor. 12:9-10). A weakness in this sense is not a sin. Nor is it the normal immaturity we leave behind as we grow closer to Christ. It is the lack of strength or ability to do something we consider desirable or necessary. It could be a physical disability, such as a speech impediment, or a personality trait we don't like, such as shyness. The apostle Paul did not tell us what his weakness was, only that it was a tormenting, demonic "thorn" in his flesh (v. 7). Perhaps if he had named his specific weakness, we might have had the tendency to glorify his weakness and minimize our own.

Many of us are distressed by our weaknesses, viewing them as permanent liabilities. But humble people see their weaknesses as opportunities for the power of Christ to rest on them. What I saw on the beach that morning was humility, the key not only to recognizing God's voice but to understanding it.

The Scripture declares that the humble hear and understand the voice of God. Among all the Old Testament prophets no one heard the voice of the Lord like Moses, for he was "more humble than anyone else on the face of the earth" (Num. 12:3-8). In fact, humility is one of the main character qualities of all the great prophets. Humility is the pathway to intimacy with God. David said it like this: "Though the Lord is on high, he looks upon the lowly, but the proud he knows from afar" (Ps. 138:6).

If we are humble, God will "look" on us, that is, be intimate with us. If we are proud, we will not hear his voice. He will deal with us at a distance.

What is humility? The dictionaries often begin by telling us what it is not—not proud, not arrogant, not haughty, not assertive and unpretentious. But what *is* it? Is humility taking a negative view of ourselves, believing that we are worthless and insignificant? Not at all. John the Baptist knew he was special. His conception was announced ahead of time by the angel Gabriel, one of only two angels named in Scripture (see Luke 1:11-20). His birth was celebrated by one of the most powerful prophetic words in the Bible (see Luke 1:67-79). He knew he had been given the greatest privilege of all the prophets. He knew he was the "voice" of Isaiah 40:3, the forerunner of the Messiah. John knew he was special, yet he was still humble.

Humility is not the denial of our attributes. It is believing in our hearts that our best qualities are not good enough to cause us to deserve God's attention, or even to gain us the lowest position of service to him. John knew that he was great, but in comparison with the Messiah he said that he was not worthy to perform the lowest act of service, to take the Messiah's shoes off (John 1:27). Humility is seeing ourselves not in comparison with one another but in the light of God's greatness.

If humility is so essential for hearing the voice of God, how do we get it? Not by reading about it.

The Desert

Humility is almost always acquired in the desert. Moses, David, John the Baptist, and Jesus all had significant training time in the desert. Everyone who is greatly used by the Lord is led into the "desert" to get humility. God even sent a whole nation to the desert for forty years to humble them, to bring them to a place of childlike dependence and gratitude (Deut. 8:1ff).

Prophetic ministry is often spectacular. Prophets can dazzle an audience, even an entire nation. Because of that, it is easy for prophets to become puffed up. The desert is the cure for both personal and prophetic pride. The greater the prophetic gifting, the greater and more severe the time in the desert will be. Welcome the desert. It means the gift of humility is being imparted and that promotion or restoration is on the way.

Jesus said that no one on earth was greater than John the Baptist (see Matt. 11:11). Why? Because no one embraced humility like John. It was not just that John began in humility, small in his own eyes when he looked up to Jesus. He embraced humility even when it meant his ministry would diminish in the presence of Jesus. He said of Jesus, "He must become greater; I must become less" (John 3:30). He knew, at the height of his popularity, that the coming of Jesus meant the end of the forerunner's ministry. Others would have been offended at the loss of their ministry. To John it seemed right.

Where did he learn to respond so humbly? In the desert.

God Is Still Using the Desert

I want to tell you about Paul Cain's desert experience because I think it may encourage you with yours. From his birth on, Paul has had a number of reasons to become a proud prophet. In fact, he told me that in his early ministry he was so confident in his prophetic gifting that he felt invulnerable. The desert saved him.

In 1929, Paul's mother, Anna Cain, was pregnant with him. She was only forty-four years old, but she was bedridden and dying. Cancer had destroyed her breasts and was also growing in her uterus. In addition, she had tuberculosis and congestive heart failure. The physicians at Dallas' Baylor Hospital could do no more for her. They sent her home to die. At midnight an angel appeared to her and told her she would not die, and neither would the child in her womb. The baby was a son, and he would live to preach the gospel in the power of the apostle Paul. He told her to name her son Paul. Anna was healed and gave birth to a son, just as the angel had said.

The angel did not mean that Paul would be a preacher, teacher, or theologian like the apostle, but rather that when Paul preached, he could expect to see some of the healing and revelatory power that characterized the apostle Paul's ministry.

Anna did not tell her son about her miraculous healing or about the angelic announcement of his birth. She knew the pride this could cause in him. She waited to tell him until the direction for his life had clearly been set.

Anna's son became a preacher as the angel had said. Healings and miracles were common in Paul's revival meetings even when he was a teenage preacher. As a young man in the early 1950s, he became prominent in the healing movement. By the end of the fifties, that movement had become corrupt. Paul was sick at heart to have ever been associated with it. The Lord made him a promise in the midst of his despair. If Paul would love the Lord rather than money or fame, and be content to let the Lord hide him, not just in a desert, but on the backside of a desert, then he would let him stand before a new breed of prophetic people. The Lord promised that the new breed would have the character to bear the power of God without being corrupted by it. Paul believed God, who gave him a sign that the promise was real. Paul's mother would not die before he began to meet the new breed. She was then in her mid-seventies. He thought his desert time would be over shortly.

The promise took effect immediately. Paul dropped off the national ministry scene and went to live in a tiny little house in a literal desert in Phoenix, Arizona. For eleven years his bed was a sofa in the living room while he cared for his aging mother. He tried pastoring a couple of churches during that time, but he failed at it. He wasn't a pastor, and the churches had no room for a prophet. Most of the time he lived hand to mouth, getting just enough preaching invitations to keep him afloat. Old friends and colleagues forgot him.

But the Lord never forgot. Sometimes the Lord would send an occasional "raven" with a gift out of the blue. And in the meetings he was able to secure, the Lord gave him greater revelation and miracles than in his previous national ministry.

The Lord just never let the reports of the meetings get very far out of the desert.

Several times death came calling for Paul's mother, and physicians said she wouldn't last more than a few days. But Paul knew they were wrong. She could not die until he met the new breed that the Lord had promised, and that had not yet happened.

By 1990, Paul felt he was seeing some of the Lord's new breed, or at least ones who had invitations to be part of the new breed. Finally, in April of that year, Anna Cain went home. She was 104 when she made her journey to heaven. It was the spring, the season of new beginnings, when Paul finally walked out of that desert.

I know angelic birth announcements and promises of a new breed sound far-fetched. It also sounds self-serving for me to tell it, since it happened to one of my friends. Can I prove any of this? We tried to get the 1929 records from Baylor Hospital and were told they no longer existed. But I have seen the miracles and talked to others who witnessed some of the earlier miracles. I have seen the Lord take Paul before leaders of countries for private audiences as he did with prophets of old.

As for the new breed, I can find promises of their coming in the Scriptures. Do they come in the last days, or might there be several new breeds to come before the last days? I don't know. I just know something more glorious is on the way, and prophets are going to play a major role.

And what about Anna's boy, now a silly old man in his seventies? Is he really anointed by God? His life fits into a scriptural prophetic pattern—angelic announcement, desert living before the real ministry begins, humility, and prophetic power. I hear the character of God's voice and see the fruit of the Spirit in Paul. And it comes in a package that is all too easy to reject.

FIVE

Understanding God's Meaning

B*lood pressure.*

From out of nowhere those words entered my mind. The woman at whom I was looking appeared perfectly healthy. She was seated in the third row on my left. I was standing on the stage, looking at the crowd, praying for revelation. And then it came, though nothing suggested the woman had blood pressure problems, and I had not been talking or thinking about illnesses.

I had grown accustomed to experiences like this, experiences that some call "words of knowledge." However, I wasn't accustomed to what was about to follow, nor was I prepared for the lesson the Lord was going to give, a lesson about how we should listen when he speaks, and more importantly, a lesson about my heart.

I looked at the woman for a moment longer. This was going to be impressive. I was sure.

"Do you have high blood pressure?" I asked the lady.

"No," she replied. I couldn't believe it. I was sure the Lord had indicated she did. Maybe I had been a little hasty in calling *her* out. Maybe it was someone in her family.

"Does anyone in your family have high blood pressure?"

"No." Strike two. Maybe the revelation wasn't for this lady, but for someone seated near her, and I just hadn't given the Lord time to indicate who it really was.

"Does anyone seated around this lady have high blood pressure?" I asked that part of the audience.

Strike three. I suppose I could have continued, "Well, does anybody know anybody anywhere in the world that might possibly have high blood pressure, or had it once upon a time?" That might have gotten me kicked off the team. If I just accepted strike three, I might get to bat again. The church where I was speaking, Trinity Fellowship of Amarillo, Texas, was one of my favorite churches. I wanted to stay on the team there. So, embarrassed and confused, I admitted my mistake and continued the meeting.

After the meeting, the woman who did not have high blood pressure came up to me and said, "You know, my husband has low blood pressure. It's so bad that sometimes he passes out. Do you think that might have been what you were seeing?" I had made a beginner's error in prophetic ministry.

The mercy of the Lord is so great that he overcame my error, so that nothing was lost that didn't need to be lost. Actually, more was actually gained in my mistake than would have been gained in my success. Before I explain the error, let me explain the mercy. First, the Lord still allowed us to identify who had the blood pressure problem so we could pray for him. Second, the Lord showed me why I made the error so that I could learn from it. Third, since I am writing about it now, you and others may profit from my failure. Fourth, there was something I needed to lose. The embarrassment I suffered was a small price to pay for that loss, which I will share with you later.

The wonderful thing I took away from this little failure was that when we are willing to risk looking foolish for the Lord, his mercy redeems even our mistakes and makes us better.

What had led to the mistake? Actually there were two mistakes. Nobody saw the first one, not even me, because it took place in a hidden part of my heart. The first mistake produced the one the audience saw, a simple flaw in my methods, which was much easier to correct than the mistake I'd made in my heart.

Revelation, Interpretation, and Application

The mistake in my method was this: I had failed to distinguish between revelation (what is said), interpretation (what it means), and application (what we do about it). These three factors are involved every time God speaks to us.

The revelation is the message of God. The message may come through the Bible, a dream, an impression, or in other ways. If the revelation is from God, then it must be true because God cannot lie (see Heb. 6:18). However, we can have a true revelation and give it a wrong interpretation. Furthermore, we can have a true revelation, a true interpretation, and a wrong application. We have to be right at all three stages if the message from the Lord is going to benefit someone.

I had heard the words "blood pressure" in my mind when I looked at the woman. The revelation was true, but my interpretation was false. I immediately jumped to the conclusion that it must mean high blood pressure. After all, high blood pressure is much more common than low blood pressure. The other assumption I made was that the revelation referred to the woman that I was looking at when the word came into my mind. Calling her out publicly (the application), ensured my embarrassment.

Here is what I should have done. I should have asked the Lord what the word about blood pressure meant and how it applied to this lady. Suppose I had done that, but the Lord had not answered me. Then I could have asked the lady to help me with the interpretation. I could have said, "Just a moment ago, I was looking at you and the words 'blood pressure' came to my mind. Do those words mean anything to you?" Had I done this, she would have said, "Oh, my! They certainly do mean something. My husband has low blood pressure, and he even passes out from it!"

Even seasoned prophetic people can misapply revelation. The prophet Agabus heard the Holy Spirit say that when Paul went to Jerusalem he would be imprisoned. Paul's companions, including Luke and maybe even Agabus, urged him not to go. But Paul went anyway (see Acts 21:10-14). The revelation was true. But Paul and his companions came up with two contradictory applications of the revelation. One of them had to be wrong.

So a helpful practice is to distinguish between the revelation, interpretation, and application.

Write It Down

Another helpful practice is to follow Daniel's example. He wrote down his visions and dreams immediately after having them (see Dan. 7:1). We cannot interpret what we cannot remember. We can have the most vivid dream and think we will never forget it. But if we do not write it down within five to ten minutes after waking, most likely we will forget the dream within the hour. Visions and impressions can also be lost quickly, as well as insights gained from meditating on Scripture. I have developed the habit of writing down everything. This has helped me to accommodate the Lord's tendency to speak to me at "inconvenient" times. I think the Lord often speaks to us at inconvenient times to test our desire to hear him.

For much of my Christian life I had no appreciation of the Lord's spontaneity. I assumed he would speak to me only through the Bible, and that it would be *when* I was studying the Bible. It just seemed reasonable to me that God would accommodate himself to my preferred mode of divine communication and to my schedule. After all, I was quite busy serving him. I made notes during my Bible study, and God did speak to me. I learned things about God, the devil and demons, myself, and others. But I also missed a great deal of what God was saying to me during those days because I restricted my listening to only one form of the Lord's communication and mainly to one time of the day.

Although God was speaking to me at various times and in various ways, I ignored those ways because I thought they were unreliable. I thought they would distract me from the Bible, even lessen my love for it. I expected God to speak to me only when I was sitting behind a comfortable desk with an open Bible, a few other books, a notepad, and a cup of hot coffee at hand. It was not very personal and not very much like the way he spoke to people in the Bible, but it was convenient. And it suited my academic personality.

When I finally decided that the way God spoke to people in the Bible was also the way he was speaking to people today, I began to hear his voice more frequently and more personally. I now have a more intimate relationship with him. Because of the intimacy in our relationship, I speak to him often during the day. And he to me. What I've discovered is that he is not nearly so predictable as I used to imagine. And that discovery has made life with him much more adventurous.

I keep paper, pen, and sometimes a little recorder with me wherever I go, and also by my bed. If I wake up at 3:00 A.M. at the end of a vivid dream, I write it down. If an insight comes to me while I'm driving, I can use the recorder to capture it. God often speaks to us during mundane chores. When he does, we need to stop and write it down. This habit will help us meditate on what he says to us. Sometimes he may show us something that will not come to pass for months or even years. Take Mary, for example.

When the shepherds came to Mary telling her all that the angels had said about her baby son, she "treasured up all these things and pondered them in her heart" (Luke 2:19). When her twelve-year-old son wandered off from the caravan to spend an extra three days at the temple, she did not understand his enigmatic excuse, but she "treasured all these things in her heart" (Luke 2:51). Years later when she needed the treasure to get her through her greatest pain, there it was safely hidden in her heart for just that day.

Paul Cain astounded all of us in a conference in 1990 when he took out a yellowed sheet of paper containing a prophecy he had received from the Lord in the 1960s about a young woman, who, as it turned out, was not even born at the time he received the prophecy. He had carried the prophecy for almost thirty years, waiting to meet the young woman. And there she was in Anaheim, California. The prophecy was a perfect fit, but it took years before she was able to try it on.

If we do not write down the revelation, we may lose the blessing that was meant for us and others. It may even cost us money, as it once did with me.

I was in the middle of some mindless task when out of nowhere an impression came into my mind regarding a stock I own. The impression was that the stock was going to triple in value, and when it did, I should sell it. I was sure this was from God. I did not write it down, but I did tell my wife. The stock began to rise until it tripled. I did not sell. I had forgotten the impression. And besides, no one thinks *their rising* stock will ever stop rising. I still own the stock today. It is back down to the price it was at the time I had the impression. My wife reminded me of the impression—after the stock fell. She also reminded me to practice what I preach. Write it down.

The Role of the Heart

Writing down your revelations as well as distinguishing between revelation, interpretation, and application are helpful practices. Still, they don't get to the heart of interpretation. For example, in the story at the beginning of this chapter, you may have wondered why God did not just say "low blood pressure" in the first place. If he could suggest "blood pressure" to my mind, how difficult would it have been to add the word "low"? Even if I had not given the revelation an erroneous interpretation, that question would still need an answer. In that answer lies the key to interpreting all revelation.

I think God omitted the word "low" because he was teaching me humility. First, he was teaching me to ask for an interpretation that I might learn the habit of humble dependence on him for everything. Second, he let me suffer a little healthy embarrassment. Let me explain why the embarrassment was healthy.

When the words "blood pressure" came to my mind, I experienced a surge of joy. In retrospect I know that part of that joy was the delight I always feel in the presence of concrete expressions of the Lord's omniscience. But another part of the joy came from anticipating how impressed the audience was about to be with *my* revelatory knowledge. I did not know I had fallen into a common trap.

"Knowledge puffs up" (1 Cor. 8:1). No one is immune from the pride of knowledge, not the scholar with his mastery of academic minutiae or the prophet who sees the secrets of others' hearts. Knowledge in any form makes it difficult for us to escape being impressed with ourselves or to escape the joy of impressing others. This does not impress the One who knows everything. He was rather hoping we would use the knowledge he gave us in a different way, to impress people with his Son. So, to help us die to the pleasure of self-exaltation he occasionally replaces that pleasure with embarrassment.

In my case, the embarrassment caused me to turn to the Lord for an explanation of my mistake. Eventually I recognized it for what it was, a gentle reminder not to be impressed with myself when the Holy Spirit shows me the secrets of his children. The embarrassment that the Lord engineered was not a sign of his irritation, but rather of his love and his commitment to instill humility in me.

Later, we shall return to the refining quality of embarrassment, but for now let me just note that you won't find it discussed in the literature dealing with the science of biblical interpretation. There is a telling reason for this omission.

Most of the books on interpreting Scripture that I have read lead you to believe that the key to understanding the Bible lies in your mind. The best interpreters know the original languages and historical backgrounds of the Bible. They understand literary structure, systematic theology, and many other things. In short, they are the intellectual elite. Of course, no one admits to holding this position, but they demonstrate it by what they do *not* say as much as by their emphasis on the mind as the key to understanding divine communication.

Please don't misunderstand. I am not denigrating scholarship. Scholarship can be a great blessing. Every time I use a concordance, a great biblical commentary, or a carefully thought-out theological monograph, I am benefiting from someone's scholarship. What I am objecting to is the intellectual pride that is too frequently found in biblical scholarship, and the pride that makes the mind the key element in our effort to draw close to God. All too often those of us who have spent considerable time in academic realms forget the purpose of all theological study: to see God in his glory, to draw close to him, and to enjoy him forever. The mind certainly has a role to play in this pursuit, but it is not the chief role.

According to the Bible, as far as human responsibility is concerned, the key to interpreting all forms of divine revelation is found in the heart, not in the mind. The religious leaders of Jesus' day studied the Bible more than anyone, but because of the condition of their hearts they never heard God's voice at any time (see John 5:37). When God spoke to Jesus in an audible voice, some of the people standing by him only heard thunder even though the voice had come for their benefit (see John 12:27-30). If our hearts are not right, we won't be able to recognize God even when he speaks to us in an audible voice.

The Pharisees may have been intelligent, but they were also arrogant. Their pride made it impossible for them to hear God's voice in the Bible, in the miracles of Jesus, or in any of the other ways God spoke. On the other hand, Jesus was humble in heart (see Matt. 11:29) and never failed to hear God's voice. Humility, not intelligence, has always been the heart quality that moves God to speak to us and enables us to hear him clearly. It is the humble, not the smart, that God guides and teaches (see Ps. 25:9).

When it comes to understanding God's voice, three expressions of humility stand out.

The humble want

- to obey,
- to be friends with God,
- and to pray.

Willing to Obey

The religious leaders did not believe that Jesus was speaking the words of God, so he gave them a way to discern the origin of his message. He said, "If any man is willing to do His will, he shall know of the teaching, whether it is of God, or whether I speak from Myself" (John 7:17, NASB).

Humble people want to obey God, even when obedience is painful. Our willingness to do whatever he tells us encourages him to speak to us and enables us to recognize and understand his voice. Why should he speak to us if he knows we have no intention of obeying him?

Friendship With God

Humble hearts are never satisfied with obedience alone. They want an intimate friendship with God. And they want that friendship more than they want a ministry. The most impenetrable mystery is that this is also what God longs for.

The Lord longs for friends with whom he can share his secrets. Abraham got so close to God that God did not want to do anything without revealing it to him first (see Gen. 18:17). This is the goal of prophetic ministry, not the delivering of prophetic words. Powerful prophetic words are the by-product of being close friends with the most powerful Word of all.

Which do you think Jesus would rather have, servants or friends? Which would you rather have? Who brings you the most joy, the person who waits on you, or the one with whom you share your heart?

Jesus said to the disciples, "I no longer call you servants, because a servant does not know his master's business. Instead, I have called you friends, for everything that I learned from my Father I have made known to you" (John 15:15). God wants friends with whom he can be intimate. What do we want?

Good friendships do not just happen. They are cultivated over a period of time, and they are often painful. They take time because trust grows slowly. They are painful because friends become vulnerable to one another, and no one can hurt us like a close friend. The pain of intimacy scares some of us into settling for just being servants. But humble people endure the pain and take the time that all great friendships require.

Ministry sidetracks me all the time. Someone has said the greatest hindrance to loving God is serving God. I believe it. I have to ask myself repeatedly: what is it I really want, a great following or a great friendship? When I am really sidetracked, I forget to ask myself that question. But then God asks me. He seems determined to make a good friend out of me in spite of my willingness to settle for less. And I am sure he feels the same way about you.

Prayer

Humble people pray. Praying is one of the most practical things we can do, both to get revelation and to understand it. God told Jeremiah, "Call to me and I will answer you and tell you great and unsearchable things you do not know" (Jer. 33:3). How much revelation do we forfeit simply because we do not ask God to tell us "unsearchable things"? How much revelation do we fail to understand because we do not ask God to reveal its meaning?

When Daniel was meditating on Jeremiah's prophecy that Israel's captivity would last for seventy years, he prayed. An angel was sent to give Daniel "insight and understanding" (Dan. 9:22). Prayer is the instrument that allows us to search the depths of Scripture, as well as the meaning of visions and dreams.

Prophets have special gifts to interpret revelation occurring outside the Bible. Some of today's prophets have gifts similar to Joseph and Daniel, who were extraordinarily proficient at interpreting not only their own dreams but also the dreams of others. Some prophets are so gifted at interpretation that it seems effortless. But if we examine the lives of those in the Bible who are skilled interpreters of revelation, we find they were always devoted to prayer. Consider Daniel again.

In the third year of King Cyrus, Daniel had a vision so perplexing and horrifying that he mourned, fasted, and prayed over the vision for three weeks. At the end of the three weeks an angel came to Daniel and said,

"Do not be afraid, Daniel. Since the first day that you set your mind to gain understanding and to humble yourself before your God, your words were heard, and I have come in response to them.... Now I have come to explain to you what will happen to your people in the future..." (Dan. 10:12-14).

This experience makes Daniel a model for all of us who want to understand the language of the Holy Spirit.

All of the elements that unlock the meaning of revelation—humility expressed in prayer, friendship with God, and willingness to obey God—can be found in this chapter of Daniel. The prophet was given a vision he could not understand. Instead of giving up, he "set [his] mind to gain understanding." Then he prayed and fasted until the interpretation came. When we pray and fast, we are confessing our weakness and expressing our dependence on God. This is why the angel said that Daniel had humbled himself before God. He had a friendship with God, for he was "highly esteemed" by God (10:19). And he was willing to do whatever was required to obey God and to understand the vision.

Following Daniel's example is the best way I know to gain understanding of divine mysteries. It does not guarantee, though, that the Lord will automatically show us the meaning of Scripture or other forms of revelation. The Lord's friendships are not bound by mechanical rules. We know so little of God and his ways. Some things he will leave shrouded in mystery regardless of our best efforts to understand them. Don't be discouraged by this. A life without mystery is a dull life. And even though mysteries may make us anxious at times, God promises to quell our anxieties with his peace (see Phil. 4:6-7). Remember this the next time the Lord speaks to you with a disturbing symbol.

The Purpose of Symbolic Language

"Unless you eat the flesh of the Son of Man and drink his blood, you have no life in you," said Jesus (John 6:53).

Why would he use such outrageous symbolism? The crowd of disciples following him did not appreciate it. It caused them to grumble, "This is a hard teaching. Who can accept it?" (John 6:60). And it caused many of them to desert him.

But why were they following him in the first place? Jesus said they were following him for food (see John 6:26). And that is the great temptation of religious people, using God rather than loving him, following him for what he can do for us rather than for who he is. The pagans went after idols for the same reason. Jesus was happy to provide food for his followers, but he wanted them to know he was more than a caterer.

Jesus transformed their desire for physical food into one of his most shocking metaphors. He was telling the crowd that they were seeking him for too little. He was not only the sustenance of physical life, but also the source of eternal life. The metaphor was meant to shock them into looking beneath the surface of the miracle of the loaves and fishes.

Jesus warned them that his words were not literal (see John 6:63). If only they had stayed around long enough, they would have learned that Jesus used hard sayings to frustrate the impure motives of everyone who tried to be close to him. But they couldn't endure the frustration. They left the Bread of Heaven to look for a food that was more down-to-earth.

When he tried to tell his followers that he was the real food, "the bread that came down from heaven," the Jewish leaders on the fringe of the crowd who overheard were offended. The Jewish leadership had fallen into the other great temptation of religious people, to serve God through merely human intellect, discipline, and traditions. This offended the Lord so much that *he* offended their understanding. He used a hard saying to conceal the key to life from the Jewish leaders.

The Lord hides his wisdom in the Holy Spirit so that the intellectually and religiously proud cannot find it with their natural talents. The ones who are committed to living by the power of their own intellects can't live with that offense to their minds.

The twelve disciples were just as clueless, but they were not offended. They believed Jesus had a purpose in using the shocking language. And they stayed around to learn what he really meant.

To sum up this section, symbolic language conceals truth from the proud, reveals the most profound truth to the humble, and jars us awake when we are tempted to use God rather than love him. It also does something else.

It impacts our emotions. This is especially true of dreams and visions, which are often symbolic rather than literal. Prosaic warnings may be easily ignored, but the symbols of dreams and visions may frighten us out of our lethargy (see Job 33:15-18). I know we preachers are always telling everyone not to live by their feelings, but our exhortations will never change the fact that our feelings influence us greatly. Because they do, God uses pictures and symbols to intensify our feelings.

Not all of God's warnings terrify us. Sometimes they show us our future, a bright future that we are in danger of losing. Such was the case with a young man in our church.

He was flirting with sexual immorality. Actually it was flirting with him in the form of several young, wild women who were pursuing him. I was not the only leader to warn him. But the warnings found no home in his heart. Now it was God's turn to provide a more direct approach. A dream.

The dreams showed the young man married and in the delivery room with his beautiful wife. A beautiful son was born and placed in his arms. His family was gathered around him. He was overwhelmed with love and exploding with joy. When he woke up, the scene lingered and so did the joy, and he understood.

God had shown him the future, his future. A marriage made in heaven was waiting for him. Now the importance of his present actions weighed heavily on him. He understood the women pursuing him could steal what he had seen, and he told them good-bye.

This dream, while prophetic, was not really symbolic, and therefore, it was easy to interpret. But how about the difficult symbols of dreams and visions? How do we interpret them?

Interpreting Symbols

When Jesus mystified everyone with the invitation to drink his blood and eat his flesh, the twelve disciples reacted differently from the crowd. Instead of deserting the Lord, they stayed close to him, talked to him, and waited for him to reveal his meaning.

Today, we do these same things through prayer. For in prayer we draw close to Jesus, talk with him, and wait upon him.

I'm now going to offer some practical suggestions for interpreting symbols, but none of the following advice comes close to the importance of prayer. Conversing with the One who gave us the symbols is the best way to discover their meaning.

Although it is possible to discern some fairly consistent symbolic meanings in Scripture as well as in contemporary experience, there is no manual of symbols that will give us *automatic* interpretations of the nonliteral elements in our dreams and visions. This is because symbols can have different meanings in different contexts. In one setting a baby may represent a new ministry filled with potential. In another the baby may represent weakness and immaturity. So, pay close attention to the context.

Even though we don't have a manual to give us automatic understanding, it is still valuable to search Scripture and contemporary experience, both of which may suggest possible meanings for the symbolic use of persons, places, things, or events.

Many things have both literal and symbolic meanings in the Bible. For example, the color purple often stands for royalty, blue for heaven or revelation. Many plants and animals have symbolic functions. Foxes can symbolize cunning or they can represent small destructive influences, as in the little problems that will destroy a marriage over time if they are ignored (Song of Songs 2:14). Vipers may represent either religious poison or gossip. Body parts have symbolic functions. The right hand stands for power. Almost anything can have a nonliteral meaning. To cite just a few more examples, wine can represent joy. Wind may represent the Holy Spirit (see John 3:8)—or it may represent judgment (see 1 Kings 19:11). Gold, silver, or jewels represent something valuable and rare.

How do we discover these possibilities? By using a concordance, preferably an electronic one. Computer software is so much faster than using a book. I can type in the word that I'm looking for, and immediately all its occurrences come onto the screen. I can scroll up and down, reading the context in which any word lies. The concordance will usually reveal several possible symbolic meanings, but frequently while I am searching, one meaning will seem to jump off the page and fit perfectly into the context of my dream or vision.

Sometimes symbols will be taken from our contemporary experience rather than from the Bible. When this happens, look for the *commonplace associations* of the symbol, that is, the thing or things that you usually think of in connection with the symbol. For example, in your dream you are in an airplane that crashes because of pilot error. You don't need a scientific knowledge of aircraft to understand this dream. What do you commonly associate with airplanes? Transportation, speed, and high altitude are the first things that come to my mind. The airplane could represent a ministry that is taking you to spiritual heights very fast, but because of the leaders' inexperience the ministry is headed for a major disaster. So, the dream could be a warning to pray for the leaders of the ministry.

Our thoughts and feelings about the symbol are important, too, for God chooses particular symbols because of their potential to communicate with us. If we lived in a remote place where no one had any knowledge of airplanes, it is not likely that he would use them as symbols to convey his truth.

Another practical tip for understanding dreams or visions is to pay attention to any detail that stands out. It will usually be a major clue to the meaning of the revelation. But don't try to get a meaning out of every detail of a symbol. The context of the dream or vision will determine which details are relevant.

Over the years, as you treasure the dreams and visions given to you by the Lord, you may find that you have acquired your own personalized dream vocabulary.

None of the above helps for interpreting symbols should be seen as minimizing or contradicting the need for prayer. When we want to understand a divine communication, whether a scriptural text or a dream, we should pray, consult others who have wisdom in this area, and make use of any scholarly resource at our disposal. We only want to be sure that our ultimate confidence is in the Lord's goodness to make his revelations clear, rather than in our intellectual capacities to figure them out.

I have spent so much time on symbolic meanings because the most common mistake made in interpreting dreams and visions is to take something literally that was intended to be taken symbolically. For example, heart attacks often speak of spiritual attacks on the heart. Wheelchairs frequently denote spiritual paralysis. A leader you know appears on a famous national TV program in your dream. This may mean that the ministry he or she represents is going to be given national exposure, not that the leader is actually going to appear on T.V. There are no rigid rules to distinguish the literal from the symbolic or to automatically decipher symbols. Discernment is acquired in prayer over time with practice.

Another bit of advice. Most of the time, negative events in dreams and visions are warnings, not decreed events (see Job 33:13-18). The dream may warn us what will happen if we do not repent of a certain attitude or behavior. Or we may not be doing anything wrong at all. Perhaps the devil has planned a special attack against us, and the negative dream is an encouragement to pray so the calamity won't come to pass. This is the way I treat all negative dreams unless the Lord shows me otherwise. One last thing about interpreting dreams.

Tormenting Dreams

She was being shot repeatedly with a machine gun. She felt every bullet rip into her flesh, but she could not fall down. The force of the shots was holding her body up. And she could not die. So, the bullets just kept tearing into her. This was one of the dreams Leesa woke up to shortly after she began to have prophetic dreams.

All prophetic people I know are subject to tormenting dreams. These dreams seem to be revelatory. They tell a very real and coherent story, but it's a bad story, usually the thing the prophetic person fears most. If a prophetess is feeling she is losing her beauty, she may have a dream about her husband being attracted to another woman. The dream will be so real that she will experience the despair of abandonment. She may even wake up angry at her husband. Sometimes the devil is the source of these dreams. He is a master deceiver and will imitate the ways that God speaks (see chapter 8, "Deception, Demons, and False Prophets").

In other instances, we ourselves are the source of the tormenting dream. What we do just before we go to bed can influence our dreams. If we fall asleep worrying, chances are we will have a negative dream about our worries. Movies we watch before we fall asleep, especially horror movies, may have a negative effect in our dreams. Excessive amounts of alcohol or certain kinds of foods can also interfere with our dreams. In addition, some kinds of drugs, legal ones as well as illegal, trouble our dreams.

How can we tell the difference between a true warning dream and a tormenting dream? First, see if there is a connection between the dream and what we were doing just before we fell asleep. Second, does the dream reflect something we habitually fear or worry about? Fear and worry are entry points for demonic deception. Third, does the dream take away our hope, making us feel that neither prayer nor repentance will help? Hopelessness and condemnation are signs of the accuser's revelation. If we consistently ask the Lord to show us the difference between his dreams and the ones of our flesh or those from the enemy, we will learn to discern the source.

When Leesa first began to have prophetic dreams, almost every other night she had a tormenting one. We put up with this for six weeks before we came to our senses. We prayed every night before we went to bed, asking God to keep the devil from invading her dreams. The invasion stopped. Occasionally she is visited by a tormenting dream, but that is part of the price of being prophetic.

Prophets do not live in a tidy world. They move in realms where angels and demons cross paths, where the counterfeit and the real intermingle. Confusion and ambiguity are their frequent companions. A fleeting vision or a barely remembered dream may hold the key for someone's rescue. Of all the gifts, none seem to rest on such flimsy experiences as prophecy. No ministry is as difficult to learn. It is so much more art than science. It may also be the most valuable of all the gifts. It is the only spiritual gift that the apostle Paul singled out and urged the whole church to pursue (see 1 Cor. 14:1, 39).

Be patient with yourself as you learn to understand the prophetic language of the Holy Spirit. Humble persistence is more important than intelligence in trying to discover what only God can reveal. Understanding is the reward for those "who because of practice have their senses trained to discern good and evil" (Heb. 5:14, NASB).

SIX

Avoiding Prophetic Craziness

Not all crazy people are in asylums. Some are running around loose, imitating prophets. Often they get away with it because some of the real prophets seem just borderline sane.

I'm not just talking about today's genuine prophets. I also mean the prophets of the Bible. If Jeremiah were ministering today, any number of churchgoing people would recommend Prozac and long-term counseling. The biblical prophets frequently not only appear unhappy and angry, but they also do strange things. Jeremiah bought an expensive linen belt, buried it, and dug it up later, claiming the ruined belt was a message to the nation. Hosea married a prostitute—not one of those sentimental prostitutes in the movies, one who has a heart of gold, but a brazen prostitute who has other men's babies. The most literate prophet of the Bible, Isaiah, went around naked for three years. What kind of therapy would we encourage him to enter if he were in our congregation?

The bizarre behavior of the biblical prophets does not bother us today because they are not in our churches. They are safely tucked away in the pages of the Bible. We are also helped greatly by the fact that the Bible is the most unread book in our churches. This means that many of us are not aware of the strange things in the Bible.

But it is not just our biblical ignorance and their contemporary absence that keeps us comfortable with the eccentric acts of the prophets. There is also a theological reason why we are not troubled by their incongruous conduct. What ultimately legitimizes the prophets of the Bible is that God stands behind their weird ways.

God is the one who told Jeremiah, Hosea, Isaiah, and company to do those peculiar things. The fact that God told Isaiah to go naked or told Abraham to kill his son can make us comfortable with Isaiah and Abraham. However, it should not make us comfortable with God. The only way to derive comfort here is to assume that God is not speaking anymore except in the pages of the Bible, or that he has given up his strange ways. But you probably would not be reading this book if you believed that. It is much more likely that you believe God is still speaking today and that he might even ask you to do something strange. If you are not humble, wise, and careful, these beliefs may very well get you into trouble that God did not intend for you.

Prophetic Megalomania

When I first began pursuing prophetic ministry, I met a young man who thought he was a prophet. I will call him Robert. He was walking along the sidewalk after a rain and noticed a dead worm in his path. He thought God was speaking to him about the worm. So he picked it up, thinking that if he prayed for it God would bring it back to life. The worm did not respond. Undaunted by his failure to revive the worm, he had a new thought. God was leading him to put the worm into an envelope and give it to one of the leaders of a prominent Christian movement.

Robert had no idea why God wanted him to do this. He also had no authority or place within the movement, but he felt like a man on a mission from God. When he walked into the offices of the ministry to deliver the deceased worm, he was not given the warmest of receptions. He interpreted this to mean that the underlings serving the leader were jealous of him and afraid that he might become closer to the leader than they were. If the underlings were afraid, their fear proved groundless when the leader opened the envelope. The leader did the right thing by the late little annelid and by the "prophet." He gave the worm an immediate burial in the wastepaper basket. Then he thanked Robert and told him good-bye.

Robert was sure that his failure to worm his way into the movement was due to the corrupt hearts of the underlings who had allowed an evil spirit access to the ministry offices. He could not see that his strange act had anything to do with his rejection. After all, the unsolicited gift of an expired earthworm is not even close to the exhibitionism of a naked prophet.

I followed the young man's career for a while longer, and the same patterns were repeated. Instead of learning from the failures of his bizarre behavior, he developed a theology to justify it. God "told" him somewhere along his journey that his ministry would be rejected. Armed with the weird incidents of the Bible and a divine promise of rejection, he would always be able to justify his antisocial ways and blame someone else for his failures in ministry. I know of at least one occasion where he turned a whole church off to the gifts of the Spirit, helping them to despise the gift of prophecy in particular.

This is sad, because Robert is not a prophet. He is a stumbling block masquerading as a prophet. Several leaders tried to help him see this, but they were not able to reach him.

In the Book of Proverbs the fool is depicted as a megalomaniac beyond correction (see Prov. 27:22). If we are foolish enough, we will always be able to find something in the Bible to justify wrong or weird behavior or corruption in our hearts.

Thankfully I have met only one or two people in the prophetic ministry as insular as Robert. However, his example is a warning: before we use the prophets of the Bible to justify some unorthodox action on our part, we should remember that they had the highest levels of discernment and character. When God commanded Abraham to sacrifice Isaac or Hosea to marry Gomer, the issue was not whether or not they were discerning accurately the voice of God. They heard his voice clearly. The issue was obedience to God. We should also expect God's voice to be that clear before doing something strange, especially when we could hurt someone.

Still, sometimes the Lord does do things that appear unorthodox or strange. But there is a right way and a wrong way to respond to these acts.

Glorifying the Strange

The Lord did transport prophets in the Spirit to other places to show them things. And sometimes the Spirit picked up people physically and dropped them off at other locations (see 1 Kings 18:12; Acts 8:39). Today all this sounds like New Age astral travel. But the Scriptures teach us that the Lord indeed does strange things. For example, he caused a donkey to speak (see Num. 22:21-30). And he must have done something strange to the apostle Paul's handkerchiefs because when people waved them over the demon-possessed, the demons came out and illnesses were cured (see Acts 19:11-12). These things actually happened, and God did them all.

Why? Sometimes to offend the mind of the religious know-it-alls, sometimes to frustrate the flesh of the proud, and perhaps for a hundred other reasons God has never cared to share with us. The point is that from the beginning to the end of the Bible, God did strange things. It would be foolish to imagine that once the Bible was completed, God changed his ways to accommodate our sense of good taste. He is still doing strange things. Which raises a question.

How should we respond when we encounter one of God's strange acts today? We should glorify him for the experience. Unfortunately, many in the church glorify the experience. Recently I was in a meeting where God had been revealing his presence with some unusual physical manifestations. Five people were giving testimonies at the beginning of the meeting. The first four told about life-changing encounters with God at this series of meetings and included humorous details of physical phenomena they had experienced. The fifth, a young lady, told how her life had been changed, but added that she had not experienced any physical manifestations.

The interviewer said to a crowd of several thousand, "See, that shows you don't have to shake or fall down to experience the power of God." Then as a group prayed on the stage for the young lady, he added, "But God's gonna get you yet." The crowd erupted into laughter and applause, hoping she would fall or shake. She didn't.

The interviewer did not mean to do it, but his last statement told the crowd that if you have not shaken, you have not really met God's power. He was glorifying the manifestations of God's presence rather than God. When we do this, we are like children on Christmas morning who unwrap our presents but play instead with the shiny wrapping paper. When God does give physical manifestations, they are just the wrapping paper around his presence. That's the real gift. It is the presence that is crucial, not how the presence is manifested.

The interviewer did not know he was glorifying the experience rather than God. Neither do we. Putting our attention on manifestations and methods always leads us into deception because our eyes have left the One who is Truth. That is why humility is so important. Humble people are less easily deceived, and even when they are deceived, they are more quickly corrected.

Reproducing the Strange

Trying to reproduce the strange can be just as damaging as glorifying the strange. Often the strange happening is a singular, sovereign event. Consider the handkerchiefs taken from Paul's body. The Bible only tells about one occurrence of this phenomenon. It happened in the city of magic, Ephesus, where people used all sorts of charms to manipulate spirits and the forces of nature. Christians, some good and some bad, try to reproduce this today by blessing prayer cloths and giving (or selling) them to the sick.

I'm not saying that God has not healed the sick today using this method—or even stranger ones. But those passing out the prayer cloths are not getting the same results as Paul did. They are copying the wrong thing. They should set their hearts on copying the character of the apostle Paul, not his handkerchiefs. When we get to the point where we do all things for the sake of the gospel (see 1 Cor. 9:23) and suffer for Christ as Paul did (see 2 Cor. 11:16-32), then, who knows, maybe God might endue our clothing with a little power. It is a lot easier to pass out prayer cloths than to get the character of Paul.

One more clue from the apostle: he talked a lot more about the Lord than he did about his strange experiences with the Lord. Paul never even mentioned the handkerchief episode. His friend Luke told that story. And Luke's purpose in telling it was not to introduce a new healing method but to demonstrate the superior power of the Lord Jesus Christ over all the Ephesian evil spirits and their magic.

In spite of the preceding cautions, at times God still does strange things. Even worse, he may do something both strange and *new*. Worse still, he may ask *us* to do something that is strange and new. What do we do then?

False Guilt

During a question-and-answer time in a recent seminar, a lady presented me with the following problem. She had been praying for a blind lady to receive her sight. Nothing happened. Then she thought of the time when Jesus spit on the ground to make mud and put it on the blind man's eyes. She felt if she would do the same, the blind lady would be healed. However, they were standing on a carpeted floor and there was not any dirt nearby. But the bigger obstacle was her fear of doing something so socially unacceptable—putting her spit and dirt in someone's eyes! Yet Jesus did it. She felt guilty for having fear. And the guiltier she felt, the more she felt he was leading her to do it. But was he? Was her hesitation due to her fear of looking foolish or to uncertainty about the leading? In the end, she didn't spit and the blind lady did not see. Now she was being tormented with guilt for not applying the mud. This happened at a conference in a foreign country, making it impractical for her to go back and pray again for the blind person using the mud method.

She asked me, "What should I have done? Was the impulse to make mud with my saliva from the Lord or from myself?"

I told her that I didn't think it was from the Lord. *First of all,* it is natural for us to think of biblical passages that correspond to our prayers for people. When I pray for blind people, the mud and spit therapy of John 9:6 almost always comes to my mind. When I pray for deaf people, I frequently wonder if I should put my fingers in their ears (see Mark 7:32). Those thoughts probably come from our familiarity with the Scriptures, not from specific divine leading. *Secondly,* when we are praying unsuccessfully for a miracle, it is natural for us to search for a reason for our failure. We may think we are not following the Bible literally enough, or we don't have enough faith, or there is sin in our life. *Thirdly,* the lady did not have certainty or peace about doing something so distasteful. She was more worried about missing God's leading than obeying God. She would have been happy to obey if she really knew it was

God leading her. Remember, when God commanded the prophets of the Bible to do something weird, he did it with such clarity that they did not wonder whether the command came from him or their emotions. *Fourthly,* this lady was relatively new at hearing God's voice and she was contemplating a prophetic act beyond her level of faith (see Rom. 12:6). These were the factors persuading me to conclude her emotions were leading her to apply the mud, not God. Since there was no clear transgression, she did not need to feel guilty.

What should she have done? She could have asked God to give her a sign that the leading was from him and not from her emotions. Or she could have included the blind lady in the decision by saying, "You'll probably think this is crazy, and I don't blame you, but I feel like doing what Jesus did—making mud with my saliva and putting it on your eyes. What do you think?" The blind lady might have said, "No way!" Or she might have said, "Well, what have I got to lose? My eyes are no good to me now anyway. Give it a try." In this way she would have been treating the blind lady as a person and not an experiment.

Ten Rules for Prophetic Success

If we obey the following ten rules we may avoid some unnecessary trouble. *Rule One:* emphasize the main and the plain, not the rare and the bizarre. Do this in your Scripture study and in your prophetic ministry. *Rule Two:* don't do anything strange without a *clear* leading from God. *Rule Three:* don't do anything prophetically that is potentially embarrassing or harmful to another person without his or her permission. If you object,

"Elijah and Elisha did not have to get permission before they did harmful things," remember, they were prophesying against God's enemies. You are ministering to his children. That is a big difference. Also remember that you are not Elijah or Elisha. When you get to their level of commitment and skill, you can have a little more latitude with rule three. *Rule Four:* repeat after me, "I am not an exception to the rules. I am a beginner in the school of the prophets." *Rules Five through Ten:* the same as Rule Four.

Strive to be as normal and unreligious as possible if you want your message to be received. That was the apostle Paul's advice (see 1 Cor. 14:23-25). Do things decently and in order, for God is a God of peace (see 1 Cor. 14:33, 40). If he wants to violate the peace, fine. But we should work to keep it.

The next chapter offers some guidelines not only for keeping the peace but also for obtaining the maximum benefit from our prophetic words.

SEVEN

Giving Prophetic Messages

For twenty minutes the insults rained down with neither tact nor mercy. But Paul Cain's expression remained unperturbed, the same quiet confidence I'd seen so many times before, radiating from his eyes as he sat absorbing the bitter berating. I could not believe this Christian leader had so little discernment and so much cruelty. I wanted to interrupt him, to speak up for Paul. Actually, I wanted to hurt him for what he was doing to my friend. But something in my friend's eyes told me to calm down. A man's life was in the balance. I remained quiet, watching for the outcome, and I'm sorry to say, hoping for judgment.

It began when a large group of ministers invited John Wimber to put on a conference in their country. John took Paul and me along. On his first night, Paul did not preach well, but he did deliver some stunning prophetic words. This, however, was not enough to satisfy one of the main organizers of the conference. He mounted a campaign against Paul to have him removed as a speaker while the conference was still in progress. The leader said to me, "We can't understand why John Wimber is letting that old Pentecostal has-been preach."

"I thought his prophetic words were incredible. And so did many in the audience," I replied.

"Well, they weren't good enough to atone for that rambling message," he said as he stormed out.

Paul heard the man's complaints without any of us relaying them. (Real prophets are not all-knowing, but they often know more than people want them to know.)

John arranged a meeting between Paul and the leader. Besides the two of them, only John and I were present. That's when the leader started the twenty-minute barrage disparaging Paul's ministerial abilities. When he finished, he said to Paul, "Do you have anything to say to me?"

"Yes, I do, but if it's OK with you, I would like to say it privately."

"Fine with me."

The two of them went into a back room. John smiled at me. He knew what was about to happen. The leader was about to learn that real prophets are scary.

When they came out, thirty minutes later, the man's demeanor had changed. He wasn't angry. He looked relieved and grateful. He said that the whole thing probably had gotten blown out of proportion. There wasn't anything that could not be smoothed over. Everything would be fine. Then he hugged Paul and would not let go for the longest time. What accounted for this transformation?

Paul had seen a sin imprisoning the leader. He had also seen that his time to repent was running out. He was a step away from being exposed and removed from his ministry, a ministry that he had faithfully built over the years, a ministry that had brought God's blessing to many. Paul could have exposed him, pronounced God's judgment on him. Instead he took him into a back room and led him to repentance.

Observing the Golden Rule

The greatest prophet once said, "Bless those who curse you" (Luke 6:28). The few who actually do that are entrusted with the greatest of God's secrets. For God knows they won't use his secrets for revenge, but rather as tools of mercy and love for reshaping damaged lives.

Paul would not tell us the sin he saw. He never does. Neither would he say what the judgment was that he saw coming, had the man not repented.

I was astounded at Paul's self-control. He listened patiently as the leader called him incompetent, incoherent, and washed up, and all the while Paul had the means to crush him, and, in my opinion, the right to do so. When I asked Paul why he had not just exposed the guy, he said that he had thought about it. But when his life was over, he really didn't care to be remembered as a great prophet. He would rather be remembered as a spiritual father. So, he just did what he thought his Father would have done. He reached out in mercy to pick up one of the little children who had stumbled.

Real prophets not only see our secrets, they are also full of mercy.

Perhaps the most important prophetic guideline is to follow the example of Paul Cain in the story above. Paul was simply following the golden rule, "Do to others as you would have them do to you" (Luke 6:31). If a prophet saw sin in your life, how would you want him to treat you? Would you want him to expose you publicly? That might make him look like a powerful prophet to some, but what would it do to you?

Those who want to look like great prophets always end up

needlessly hurting others. The prophets who are truly great treat people as they want to be treated. When they have a warning or blessing for someone, they ponder how to give it so it will achieve the maximum benefit to all. They don't just consider the way in which to deliver the message, but the timing of its delivery as well.

Getting the Timing Right

We may have a real revelation, with the right interpretation, then deliver the message without any benefit being realized because we gave it at the wrong time. A wise prophet knows that "a word aptly spoken is like apples of gold in settings of silver" (Prov. 25:11), a work of art that brings joy to the speaker and good to the hearer (see Prov. 15:23).

Never give a prophetic word to someone without asking and receiving the Lord's permission first. I am often asked, "How do we know if we have the Lord's permission to give the word?" The answer is, he will tell us if we ask him. Why would God give us a revelation and not instruct us in how to use it? If we had the capacity to receive the revelation, we also have the capacity to hear what to do with it.

We also need the Lord to show us how to apply the revelation. We need that as much as we needed him to give us the revelation and its interpretation. People are different, and, therefore, the same truth may need to be applied in different ways if it is going to benefit the hearer. An application that would needlessly provoke one person may be just right for another. The Holy Spirit must illumine each step of the process if we are ever to be a blessing to anyone.

Sometimes the Lord does not give the prophet an interpretation or application of a revelation, but he still has him speak the revelation. In this case, the Lord may be testing the hearts of the hearers to see if they value his word enough to seek him for its meaning and application. We have to be careful not to say more than God has said. If we add anything, we should distinguish between the revelation and our own opinions regarding its meaning and application. Our opinion may be valuable, but if we carelessly lead our hearers to believe it is what God has said, it will probably be deceptive.

Realizing the Power of a General Word

General words, unclear words with hundreds of appropriate applications, also tempt prophets to add to revelation. They tempt prophets because people value specific words more than general ones, and just adding a few details may make the prophet appear more powerful. But don't do it. If the general word is from the Lord, it will have power. Adding to it will only dilute it or ruin it.

Recently I was speaking to an audience on hearing God's voice. The word "dreams" flashed into my mind as I looked at a lady in the third row. That was it, just the word "dreams." I felt I was supposed to speak to the lady, but the word was just too general. I needed to improve it. In front of everyone I asked her if she had been praying to have dreams. In front of everyone, she said no.

About five minutes later, she raised her hand. She told us she had read one of my books about two weeks previous and had starting having vivid dreams. She did not have anyone to talk to about what was happening to her. She asked God to let us meet so she could ask me about the meaning of her dreams. She had no idea I was coming to her city. She found out about the meeting just in time to attend that day.

This was a divine appointment, and the Lord had even given me the subject of our meeting, her dreams. I almost spoiled it by trying to improve a general word. I should have simply said to her, "When I looked at you the word 'dreams' flashed into my mind. Does that mean anything to you?" Then she could have told her story. How much more powerful that would have been!

Being Kind

The Lord was so kind to give that lady dreams and then to arrange the meeting for which she asked. His kindness is the standard for all prophetic ministry. When we give people words, we should make them feel at ease. Smile at them. Call them by name. Always give prophetic words with tenderness and humility. We want people to feel the Lord's kindness and love through us.

Angry, self-righteous, judgmental, and accusatory messages rarely do anyone any good. I know that the Old Testament prophets frequently spoke angry words from God. These words were spoken to a rebellious people given over to idolatry or to religious hypocrisy. Jesus reserved his angry words for self-righteous, hypocritical, religious leaders (see Matt. 23). If

God has an angry message for the church today, I would expect it to come the way it has always come, from a humble, broken-hearted prophet who loves the church and identifies with its sin, and who moves at the highest level of revelation (cf. Dan. 9:4-19). Most of the angry "prophetic" words I hear today flow out of a stream of unhealed anger in the prophet's heart.

Give all messages, especially negative ones, with gentleness and tact. Don't just blurt out to a husband that his pride, self-ishness, insensitivity, and blindness will ruin his marriage. He won't receive it. He'll think you are just attacking him, taking his wife's side. Instead, say, "I know that your wife is angry and depressed. But I can see the devil is using her unhappiness to set a trap for you. He's going to try to make you think that you have nothing to do with her unhappiness, that all the serious problems in your marriage are really her fault. If you fall into the trap, you'll end up miserable for life or divorced. I think the Lord has shown me how you can escape the trap, if you care to hear it." A message shaped liked this has a chance of being heard and saving a marriage.

All prophets would do well to ask the Holy Spirit to write the following proverbs on their heart:

A gentle answer turns away wrath, but a harsh word stirs up anger.   PROVERBS 15:1

Through patience a ruler can be persuaded, and a gentle tongue can break a bone.   PROVERBS 25:15

If we frame our messages tactfully, avoiding frontal attacks on a person's character, our words are more likely to find a home in the hearts of our hearers.

Interceding

In the center of heaven there are hundreds of millions of angels. In the midst of the angels are twenty-four thrones with twenty-four elders sitting on them. In the midst of the thrones are four living creatures flying around a single throne, which is encircled by an emerald rainbow. In the center of that throne, in the very center of heaven, sits the Lord Jesus Christ. The whole heavenly entourage gazes on the beauty of that glorious Person and sings his praises nonstop (see Rev. 4–5). What is *he* doing?

He does not let the splendor of angelic adoration distract him from his main task. Hour after hour he is laboring in prayer for you and for me and for all those he is drawing to his Father (see Heb. 7:25). The greatest Prophet is also the greatest Priest, and though he is all-knowing and all-powerful, he is still praying.

Following in the Spirit of Jesus, great prophets have always been great interceders. If we truly want our prophetic word to draw our hearers to God, then we should pray for them after we deliver the message. Intercession is hard work. Actually it is easier to do anything besides praying. But it may be our prayers, not our message, which the Lord uses to help the person. It is not our job to make the person accept the word, nor is it our job to make the word come to pass. After Isaiah delivered one of his most difficult messages of judgment, he said, "I will wait for the Lord, who is hiding his face from the house of Jacob. I will put my trust in him" (Isa. 8:17). Follow Isaiah's example: wait for the Lord, and put your trust in him so you won't fall into the rejected prophet syndrome.

Withholding Words

Daniel was not only a prophet, he was a wise prophet (see Ezek. 28:3). When he received one of his most spectacular and troubling visions, he kept it to himself (see Dan. 7:28). He did not need to prove that he was a spectacular prophet by sharing the vision, even among his intimate circle. He did not get upset when God gave him a vision and then refused to let him share it. He knew the reward was the same for sharing or withholding revelation as long as either was done in obedience to the Lord.

The discipline to be silent when God is silent or when he has withheld permission to speak is a sign of prophetic maturity. God does not reveal his secrets to blabbermouths but to those who fear him (see Ps. 25:14). In heaven a prophet may be known more for what he does not say than for what he does. No one gets to the highest level of prophetic ministry without mastering the skill of prophetic restraint.

These are the prophets who can be trusted with revelation that is not yet ripe for sharing, that must be "sealed" for a later use (see Isa. 8:16; 29:11; Dan. 8:26; 12:4, 9). These are the prophets to whom God can show great secrets, then trust them *never* to repeat what they heard or saw to anyone (see 2 Cor. 12:4; Rev. 10:4). These are the trusted friends of God who have his interests at heart, not theirs.

Why would God show a prophet something and not give him permission to share it? Maybe he is calling the prophet to intercede instead of prophesy. In fact, *unless the Lord says otherwise, every revelation is also a call to prayer.* Maybe the timing for the message is not yet right. Sometimes the Lord gives a message in stages, and the prophet who speaks a partial message as if it were the whole message may lead someone astray.

It is also possible that we may see accurately what someone is planning to do, but not what God actually wants that person to do. If we speak without God's permission, we may confirm man's plans rather than God's. In that case we will have become part of the deception instead of part of the deliverance.

Saying "Thus Says the Lord"

Should you introduce your prophetic message by saying, "Thus says the Lord"? The Old Testament prophets frequently did. The New Testament counterpart is, "The Holy Spirit says" (Acts 21:11). When the prophets used this phrase, they were claiming to speak the precise words of God, not their interpretations or applications of the revelation they had received. "Thus says the Lord" allowed no debate. It meant, "This is exactly what God has said. The matter is settled." The prophets who used this phrase were not usually speaking words of personal prophecy. They had been given divine authority to speak God's words over nations. They had proven character and track records. Most were persecuted, and some became martyrs. In my opinion, we should be quick to copy their passion for God, and slower to use their vocabulary.

When we say "Thus says the Lord" to someone, we have left the person no room to disagree. He or she may feel controlled or manipulated because it is intuitively obvious, even if they can't express it, that we don't have the same authority as the prophets who spoke over nations. I am not saying that it is always wrong to use "Thus says the Lord," just that most of us using it do not have the authority to use it. Even the prophets I know who have the most authority rarely use the phrase.

On the other hand, I know good prophets who disagree with me on this issue. They use the phrase constantly when they prophesy. And I'm not going to let their style of prophesying cause me to lose the blessing of their friendship or ministry.

Prophetic Authority

Prophetic words are always subject to the authority of Scripture. In the Old Testament, even if a prophetic word came true and was confirmed by miraculous signs, it was not to be followed if it contradicted the teaching of Scripture (see Deut. 13:1-5). During Isaiah's time people were consulting mediums and spiritists. Isaiah set forth a standard to distinguish the true prophet from the false: "To the law and to the testimony! If they do not speak according to this word, they have no light of dawn" (Isa. 8:20).

Paul addressed the same problem in Corinth, where some claimed that they were led to ignore his teaching due to their own prophetic inspiration. He wrote, "If anybody thinks he is a prophet or spiritually gifted, let him acknowledge that what I am writing to you is the Lord's command" (1 Cor. 14:37).

The authority of Scripture is universal, for all people and for all times. Personal revelation is only for the people to whom it is given and only for that particular time.

How much authority should we assign to personal prophetic words? Should we expect someone to base a decision on a prophetic word that we have given? Jeremiah certainly expected the people to base their decision on his prophetic word. When the people asked him whether they should stay in Judah or flee to Egypt, he said the Lord would only protect them if they stayed in Judah (Jer. 42). The people did not listen and most of them died under judgment in Egypt. But we would be wrong to use Jeremiah or any of the Old Testaments prophets as our normal model for the authority of today's personal prophetic words. Here is why.

The Old Testament examples of prophetic ministry do not include very many instances of prophets giving "personal" words. Almost all the examples deal with prophets giving corporate words.

Even the prophet's personal words to the king were actually corporate words because their purpose was to help the king guide the nation. And it would be an error to use corporate examples as a model for personal words. In a corporate word, the prophets represented the voice of God to a nation that acknowledged him as their only ruler. In the example above, Jeremiah is not speaking to an individual to give him some guidance about where he should live. He is speaking to the remnant of the rebellious nation telling them the only way God will allow their survival.

God used the prophets to say things that neither the king nor the nation wanted to believe. In order to help the people believe, he established the prophets' authority in unforgettable ways. He came down in a cloud to speak with Moses in front of all the people (see Ex. 19:9). He caused the waters of the Jordan to stop and stand up in a heap so that the people would follow Joshua into the Promised Land (see Josh. 3:7-17). He gave extraordinary accuracy to Samuel so that none of his words fell to the ground (see 1 Sam. 3:19). He confirmed Elijah's words by withholding rain for three and a half years and by granting him the power to call down fire from heaven (see 1 Kings 17:1; 18:36-38). Divine visitations, signs from nature, great accuracy, miracles, and other supernatural experiences were the calling cards of the Old Testament prophets.

When Jesus came, he gave this authority to the apostles, not to the prophets. The authority structure of the church differs from that of the nation Israel.

The apostles, not prophets, have translocal authority in the body of Christ. The New Testament apostles gave corporate words to the whole church. God revealed to each apostle where his sphere of authority lay, and the church recognized that authority. Peter had authority among the Jews. Paul's sphere was among the Gentiles. New Testament prophets differed from their Old Testament counterparts by having a much greater ministry in personal rather than corporate words. Prophets in the church speak to individuals for their comforting, encouraging, and strengthening (see Acts 15:32; 1 Cor. 14:3). They can also give corporate words (see Acts 11:27-30), but the New Testament emphasizes their ministry to individuals.

On the local level, the elders of individual churches, not the prophets, have authority. Most New Testament prophets are not elders or leaders. Paul wrote that it is "the elders who direct the affairs of the church" (1 Tim. 5:17). And here is a critical point: *all New Testament authority is given to direct the affairs of the church, not individuals' personal lives.* When the leaders of a church or a Christian movement start to exert authority over the personal lives of their followers, they are on the road that leads to a cult. Neither prophets nor pastors should be making our personal decisions for us.

Jesus has given us a more intimate relationship to the Father than the saints of the Old Testament were able to experience. The normal experience for us is to hear his voice (see John 10:4). We have the Holy Spirit to lead us (see Rom. 8:14). He expects us to hear from the Spirit regarding our personal decisions. This does not mean that prophets cannot help us. They can support, confirm, or clarify what we think the Lord is saying to us. They can cause us to pray about directions we had not thought about. But they should never cause us to give up our privilege of hearing God's voice for ourselves. We should never act solely on someone else's light. God will hold each of us accountable for our decisions. He will never allow us to exscuse our bad decisions by saying "It was that prophet you gave me!"

This does not mean that New Testament prophets do not speak powerful and authoritative words. In fact, at the end of the age there will be a prophetic revival. The two most powerful prophets are yet to come, and their authority will be established like that of the prophets of old (see Rev. 11:3-12). Even now there are indications that God is preparing the church to receive a higher level of prophetic ministry.

Respecting Pastoral Authority

Recently I met a young man at a conference who was kind, sincere, and prophetically gifted. He felt his church had fallen into a rut and that the Lord had shown him the way out. He told the pastor that he should shut the church down for a month so they could all really learn how to do church. He could not understand why the pastor rejected him and his word.

I have no doubt that the young man saw some wrong patterns of ministry in his church. But his failure to respect the authority of his pastor undermined the effectiveness of any message he might have heard from the Lord. How did he fail to respect pastoral authority?

First, he gave a major correction without tact. He gave no thought to the impact of his message on the pastor. He did not realize he was telling his pastor that his entire previous ministry at the church was severely flawed. This was not a proper way to approach someone who had been given not only authority to direct the affairs of the church (see 1 Tim. 5:17), but also authority to watch over the young man's soul (see Heb. 13:17).

Second, he gave a message he had no authority to give. Messages that involve radical redirection of a ministry are usually entrusted to prophets who have a proven supernatural track record and acknowledged divine authority. The young man had neither.

The beginner prophet standing before me was a successful businessman who had never received any ministerial or prophetic training. I asked how he would like it if someone with no business experience told him to shut down his business for a month so he could really learn how to do business. He got the picture, but he got it too late. The damage already had been done.

And yet he is a good man, with a real gift, able to take correction. I would love to have him in my church to train him and put him to work. He just needs a better understanding of God's authority.

The purpose of divine authority is different from earthly authority. It is given to lead people into a deeper intimacy with Jesus, not to control others. Unlike earthly authority, it is given differently. Divine authority eludes those who seek it, leaves those who abuse it, and rests on those who rest in the Word.

EIGHT

Deception, Demons, and False Prophets

We were spellbound. How could this guy know the secrets of our hearts without ever having met us? There were twelve of us sitting in a circle. Most of us were pastors. Only one was a prophet. He prophesied over three of us in succession with perfect accuracy about our past and present, then told us about our future. We believed him. Turning to a fourth one, he said that in the last days the believing church in America would be divided into twelve tribes and that these twelve tribes would have great power. Looking straight at the pastor, he said, "And you are going to be the leader of one of these twelve tribes."

I should have known immediately that this was wrong. Not because the pastor had only about forty people in his church. Not because he did not move in any of the supernatural gifts of the Holy Spirit. And not because he lacked the relational skills to lead great numbers. But because when he heard the prophecy, he smiled a welcoming smile. If he had possessed the heart for such a calling, he would have *trembled* instead.

The prophecy had immediate destructive effects in the pastor's life. To mention only one, it made him think more highly of himself than he should have. After all, had not the Lord said that he would rule over a tribe in the last days?

A year later, in the inevitable descent toward disaster, the pastor asked the prophet why things were plummeting. To his credit, the prophet told the pastor he had been wrong in his prophecy. Well, sort of. What he actually said was, "I'm laying down the prophecies I gave about movements last year."

Why would a pastor believe a wrong prophecy about himself? As I got to know this pastor, I formed my own opinion of why he believed this one. Buried in his soul was a deception that organized his values and practices, acting as a filter to interpret much of his experience. The deception was that he would find significance in this life only by becoming a great leader in the church, or, more accurately, by being *recognized* as a great leader by the church. The prophecy had agreed with the deception and had moved right into a home already furnished for it.

How could such a gifted prophet miss it so badly? Did his error mean he was a false prophet? Before we can answer these questions, we need to consider the broader context of counterfeit ministry.

The Counterfeit Ministry

The devil cannot create. Only God can create. Therefore, in his fight against God, one of the devil's main strategies is to deceive people by counterfeiting what God does. Does the Lord speak to his people and lead them? So does the devil. Does the Lord give wisdom to his people? The devil has his own wisdom, which he attempts to impart to the church (see

James 3:15). Does the Holy Spirit speak to us about our sin and convict us (see John 16:8)? So does the devil. But instead of convicting, which might lead to hope, he accuses and condemns, which leads to despair (Rev. 12:10).

The devil has false christs and false apostles whom he empowers to do counterfeit signs, wonders, and miracles (see Matt. 24:24; 2 Cor. 11:13-15; 2 Thess. 2:9; Rev. 16:14). He has false prophets to whom he may impart a "lying spirit" to deceive a king (see 1 Kings 22:21) or through whom he may impart a "spirit of divination" to predict the future with some degree of accuracy (see Acts 16:16). He can provide a counterfeit anointing (see 1 John 2:27). This anointing provides false teachers and false elders with false humility, false knowledge, and false doctrines (see Acts 20:29-31; Col. 2:18, 23; 1 Tim. 6:3-5; 2 Pet. 2:1–3, 20).

These teachers and elders "abandon the faith and follow deceiving spirits and things taught by demons" (1 Tim. 4:1). In this way the devil can introduce demonic doctrines into the church. The devil also sends false brothers into the church to steal the children's bread and betray its leaders (see 2 Cor. 11-26). The devil will attempt to counterfeit everything God does, even the gifts God has given to the church.

Why does Satan want to substitute false ministry for the real ministry of the Holy Spirit? First, he knows there are many religious people who would never knowingly follow evil. Therefore, he produces an appealing counterfeit to lead the religious away from the truth. Those who are drawn to the counterfeit ministry still think they are serving God. In fact, they think the true worshippers are the ones who are deceived.

Second, if the devil can infiltrate the church with false ministers and doctrines, he can cause division, weakening the purity and power of the church. Third, by empowering counterfeit ministers with false gifts, the devil has made the church afraid of real supernatural gifts and those who use them. He has been so successful with this strategy that part of the church has more confidence in Satan's ability to deceive them than in Jesus' ability to lead them.

False Prophets

False prophets have power. They can predict the future and perform signs and wonders (see Jer. 23:10; Isa. 44:25; Matt. 7:21-23; 24:24). They seek to undermine true prophets, and when an opening comes, they persecute them (see Jer. 23:1-17; 1 John 4:6). False prophets tell people wonderful things are coming when the true prophets have decreed judgment (see Jer. 23). They live in and promote immorality among God's people (see Jer. 23:14; Rev. 2:14, 20-23). They deny foundational truths of the faith (see 2 Pet. 2:1-3). But the core element, the defining characteristic of false prophets, is that they use their power to lead people away from the true God to false gods (see Deut. 13:1-5; Jer. 23:13; Acts 13:6-8).

A false prophet is not a prophet who makes a mistake in a prediction. Deuteronomy 18:15-22 is used by some to teach that if a prophet made a mistake he was considered a false prophet and stoned. But the text from Deuteronomy is not about prophets in general. In verse 15, Moses predicts, "The Lord your God will raise up for you a prophet like me from among your own brothers." The key to understanding the prophecy is the phrase "like me." Moses was unique among all the prophets (see Num. 12:6-8; Deut. 34:10-12). As mediator of the Old Covenant, Moses stood between the people and God, as a representative of both. When he told the Israelites that God would give them "a prophet like me," he was referring to the Messiah, and this is exactly how the New Testament understood the prophecy (see Acts 3:17-26; 7:37). The false prophet of Deuteronomy 18:20 was to be put to death not because he made a mistake, but because he presumed to be like Moses, all the while attempting to lead the people to other gods.

Furthermore, there is no other text in the Old Testament supporting the idea that a prophet was executed for a mistake, and no example of the people ever applying Deuteronomy 18:15-22 in this way. On the contrary, when Nathan made a mistake by speaking in the name of the Lord to David and telling him to go ahead with his plans to build the temple, God simply corrected Nathan. No one called him a false prophet or attempted to stone him (see 2 Sam. 7:1-17).

Jesus said we recognize a false prophet by the fruit of his ministry, not by his power, his miracles, or his accuracy (see Matt. 7:15-23). And if New Testaments prophets could not make mistakes, why did Paul command the church to judge prophetic words (see 1 Cor. 14:29, NASB)?

Two contemporary theologians, both of whom I admire, have an ongoing debate. One uses the Bible to prove that the supernatural gifts of the Holy Spirit have passed away. The other uses the Bible to prove that they are still being given today. Both speak their views publicly in the name of the Lord. Since they are teaching contrary doctrines, one of them has to be teaching false doctrine. But no one I know would ever consider calling either one of them a false teacher. All teachers, pastors, and evangelists make mistakes. Even the apostle Peter made such a serious mistake that he was leading the believers in Antioch into hypocrisy, and Paul had to rebuke him publicly (see Gal. 2:11-21). Why can't we show prophets the same mercy? Why should prophetic ministry be the only ministry that is not allowed a single mistake or not allowed to grow in grace?

New Testament Categories of Prophets

The common tendency is to think of all prophetic ministry as either false or true. This is a mistake that we compound by making one of the stellar prophets of the Bible such as Isaiah or Elijah the model for all prophetic ministry today. The stellar prophets do not represent average prophetic ministry. The average is found in the schools of anonymous prophets in the Old Testament and in the gift of prophecy given to ordinary believers in the New Testament. What if we made the apostle Paul the model for all teaching, and refused to accept anyone as a teacher in the church today unless he or she could stand shoulder to shoulder with Paul? If we were to set such a standard, we would conclude that there are no teachers in the church today.

I am not saying we should not have high goals. The life and ministry of Jesus should be our goal, as well as the lives and ministries of his greatest servants. But if we take the greatest in any category of ministry and say this is the standard by which we judge whether a ministry is true or false, we will have to conclude that most ministries are false.

Two of my goals are to love Jesus like the apostle John and to teach like the apostle Paul. I am a long way from those goals. I may never reach them, or even get close. That does not mean the love I do have for Jesus is not real or that my gift of teaching is counterfeit.

When evaluating New Testament prophets, we should be thinking in New Testament terms. For example, Paul described some Christians as "spiritual," and others as "carnal" (KJV), "fleshly" (NASB), or "worldly" (NIV, 1 Cor. 3:3). Spiritual believers are those who have so consistently walked with Christ that their lives reflect the fruit of the Spirit (see Gal. 5:22-23). The carnal believer has had enough time to become spiritual but has remained immature because he has refused correction. He is better at blaming than repenting. There are also believers who are immature simply because they are new Christians who haven't had the time to mature.

Why not think of prophets in these same categories? There is the spiritual prophet who is mature in his gifting and his character. There is the immature but growing prophet whose character and gifting are improving. There is the carnal prophet who may be very gifted, but whose character deficiencies are producing more strife than the fruit of the Spirit. In terms of gifting, the immature prophet and the carnal prophet may look similar. It is only by the spiritual gift of discernment or by evaluating their ministries over time that we can distinguish between them. Finally, there is the false prophet who has a supernatural gift but is not born again, and who uses his gifting to lead people away from the Lord.

False or Carnal Prophets?

Jesus warned that at the end of the age "many false prophets will appear and deceive many people" (Matt. 24:11) and that they will have extraordinary, supernatural power (see Matt. 24:24). It is possible that the New Age movement is the beginning of the fulfillment of Jesus' warning. So far, I have not encountered many false prophets within the church. I find carnal prophets to be a much greater problem there than false prophets. But as the prophetic ministry becomes more established, we should expect to see more prophetic counterfeits. This will be a sign that the end of the age is drawing near.

Recognizing False Prophets

How do we recognize the counterfeit? Jude 4–19 is perhaps the best single passage describing false ministers. At the top of Jude's list is that they "deny Jesus Christ" (verse 4). Their motives for ministry can be found in "the way of Cain," anger and rejection; or in "Balaam's error," greed and immorality; or in "Korah's rebellion," jealousy of God's anointed leaders (verse 11). Their ministry will be characterized by immorality, rejection of authority, selfishness, manipulation, grumbling, faultfinding, flattery, empty boasting, and the disappointment of all who trust them. They are unregenerate, for they "do not have the Spirit" (verse 19). Jude's description fits not only false prophets but also false apostles, teachers, and elders.

In order to identify the counterfeit with certainty, look for two things to occur in combination. First, the counterfeit ministry will deny the written word of God. The denial won't involve a debatable matter of interpretation, but rather a foundational doctrine of the Bible. Secondly, since the devil cannot produce the fruit of the Spirit, the false minister will be devoid of spiritual life and fruit. You would think that from this fruitlessness and lifelessness it would be easy to identify false prophets. But it isn't.

False ministers are deceptive about what they believe. They are also winsome in their deception. What makes it even more difficult is that they have a degree of power that seems to validate them. With that combination they build a base of support before they reveal their true character and beliefs. Jesus warned us that their deceptive power would be so great in the last days that they could "even deceive the elect—if that were possible" (Matt. 24:24). The best way to spot their false anointing is with the discernment that comes from the true anointing. We have been given the Holy Spirit "that we may understand what God has freely given us" (1 Cor. 2:13) and reject the counterfeit gifts of the devil. In particular, the Lord has given some in the body the gift of "distinguishing between spirits" (1 Cor. 12:10). They can discern the difference between the work of the Holy Spirit, demonic spirits, and simply human spirits.

In light of the previous discussion, we would have to conclude that the prophet at the beginning of this chapter who gave the mistaken prophecy was not a false prophet. He did not deny foundational doctrines and was not leading people away from God to other gods and into immorality. Still, how could he be so stunningly accurate with three people in a row and miss it so badly with the fourth?

Open Doors for Demonic Deception

Can an evil spirit deceive a true prophet? Without getting into the debate of whether or not a Christian can be demonized, let me list some ways in which any believer can be influenced by demons. The Bible teaches that prolonged voluntary sin in one of the following areas will give the devil a place of influence in our lives:

1. Anger and unforgiveness (Eph. 4:26-27; 2 Cor. 2:9-11)
2. Lust, sexual immorality, or perversion (1 Cor. 5:5)
3. Hatred and violence (Luke 9:54-56 [KJV]; John 8:44)
4. Envy, jealousy, and selfish ambition (James 3:13-18; 1 Sam. 18:8-11)
5. Occult practices (Lev. 19:31; Deut. 18:9-13; Acts 16:17-18)
6. Idolatry or greed (1 Cor. 10:20; Rev. 9:20; 1 Tim. 6:9; Col. 3:5)
7. Blasphemy (1 Tim. 1:20)

When a prophet holds any of these within his heart, demonic powers have a chance to distort his genuine revelatory insights or even to give him a counterfeit revelation.

Was the prophet deceived by a demon when he gave the pastor that wrong prophecy? I don't think so. There are other sources of deception besides evil spirits, and I believe the answer lies there.

Prophetic Contamination From Ourselves

We don't need a devil to be deceived. Our own hearts are "deceitful above all things and beyond cure" (Jer. 17:9). We are actually prone to lie to ourselves. And remember, when we are trying to hear from God, we are always dealing with three levels: revelation, interpretation, and application. We may mistake our own thoughts for God's revelation, or we may have a true revelation and give it a wrong interpretation or application.

What contaminates this process?

The Lord promises to give us the desires of our heart as long as we delight in him (see Ps. 37:4). When we delight in something more than him, our desires lead us astray. Paul expressed this principle in Romans 8:5: "Those who live according to the sinful nature have their minds set on what that nature desires; but those who live in accordance with the Spirit have their minds set on what the Spirit desires." The normal state of growing Christians is to set their minds on God, delighting in him. But when a lapse occurs, our desires become our enemies. They deceive us (see Eph. 4:22), corrupt us (see 2 Pet. 1:4), and "choke the word, making it unfruitful" (Mark 4:19). So a wrong desire can contaminate the process of discerning God's voice.

One of the deadliest desires is the desire for prominence. This desire can make it impossible to hear the voice of God (see John 5:37, 44).

Sinful attitudes such as fear and judgmentalism also obscure revelation. For example, when I judge my brother, my vision can get blurred to the extent that I no longer see the enormity of my own sin (see Matt. 7:3-5). If a prophet has a negative dream or vision about a believer with whom he is angry, he should jettison it along with the other soulish garbage that is polluting his revelatory gift (see James 1:20).

Sometimes a prophet will go through a season in which he expends greater effort in cultivating his gift than in cultivating an intimate relationship with the Lord. Instead of pursuing a relationship, he is perfecting a ministry. Of course, this also happens to pastors, teachers, and evangelists. The results are predictable. Not only do we lose joy and peace in our personal lives, but, ironically, we also lose power in our ministry. In the case of the prophet, this means a loss of revelation or a contamination of it.

No one is exempt from cultural influences. This is another source of contamination. Sometimes unconscious cultural beliefs affect what a prophet thinks God may be saying. Or he may be so impressed by the latest theological theory floating around that he tries to accommodate what he is hearing from the Holy Spirit with the new theory.

And there is always, *always* the pressure of the people. It is so difficult for some prophets to resist the temptation to please the people, especially when a prophet regards the person standing before him as important or influential. I have seen mature prophets drop everything and rush to the powerful, assuming that an invitation from the powerful one is the same as an invitation from the All-Powerful One, only to return disappointed. The great prophets of the Bible were not impressed by the kings who ruled the earth, but rather by the King who ruled heaven and earth.

The prophet who was so accurate with me but so wrong with the other pastor had, I believe, fallen into the trap of pleasing the powerful. Not that he thought the pastor sitting before him was all that powerful, but he thought the pastor was well connected to some who were. If he impressed the pastor, maybe the pastor would use his influence to improve the prophet's connections. Perhaps this was not the cause for the error. But there has to be some cause, and after thinking about it for a long time, this is the explanation that makes the most sense to me.

The apostle Paul summed it up like this, "If I were still trying to please men, I would not be a servant of Christ" (Gal. 1:10). Paul knew that one of the quickest ways to fall into deception was to try harder to please men than to please God.

How do prophets avoid deception? The same way as all other believers: by trying to please God rather than men, by delighting in him above everything else, and by loving him more than all else, especially more than our ministries.

NINE

Growing in Your Prophetic Gift

S tanding on a stage in front of a thousand people, I was about to be humiliated. I never saw it coming. Instead, I saw a glorious revelation that would set someone free from years of pain. The revelation turned out to be from God, but so did the humiliation.

A denominational church had invited me to speak two nights in a row, the first night on hearing God and the next on healing. This was a little bit of a stretch for the church since I was not a member of that denomination and since hearing God and healing were controversial topics within that denomination.

I took an accomplished prophet with me. The message on hearing God went well. Then came the demonstration time. (You can't just talk about God speaking without giving him an opportunity to speak and the people an opportunity to hear.) We all bowed our heads and waited silently. I received a strong impression and decided to go first. I pointed to the back of a full auditorium and said, "There is someone in the back and on my right who has migraine headaches. Actually, you're having one right now. If you'll come down to the front, I think the Lord will heal you."

My mind pulsed with confidence. I was so at ease because I was sure this was from the Lord and that he would heal the person. The seconds ticked by and nobody moved. I repeated the word. Still nobody moved. As my confidence evaporated, beads of sweat formed on my temple. The people were giving me those pained looks of pity that said, *Oh, the poor teacher. He was doing so well until he tried to be a prophet.*

Somewhere between the beads of sweat and the looks of pity, my mind shut down. I was reduced to a dummy, standing on the stage beside a real prophet. My prophet friend, Phil Elston, had mercy on me. He pointed to five men in the second row and said, "Do you know what you five men have in common? You're all pastors. And you're from a denomination that wouldn't approve of your being in a meeting like this."

It was true. Phil went on to deliver a prophetic message to these five men he had never seen before. The audience was astonished. They forgot about my failure as they listened to Phil tell them the secrets of their hearts.

After the meeting, I was standing down at the front, praying for people. A young man about twenty years old came up to me and said, "That was the most amazing thing I've ever seen!"

"What thing?" I asked.

"You pointed right at me where I was sitting in the back row and said, 'Someone back there has migraines and you're having one right now.' You were pointing right at me! I've had migraines for several years, and I was having one right then. How could you have known?"

"Wait a minute. You saw me pointing right at you and you didn't come down like I asked? Why not?"

"I don't know. I've never been in a meeting like this, with all these people. I guess I was just too scared."

"What happened to your migraine?" I asked.

"That's the other amazing thing. As soon as I started walking toward you, it left. They never just go away like that. I think I'm healed!"

Accepting the Lord's Discipline

I was right about the migraines, but to all the people it looked as if I had failed. I was coming back the next night, so I could set the record straight if I wanted. Should I? What would my motives be in setting the record straight? To bring glory to God or to me? To redeem his reputation or mine?

What if God were the one who had orchestrated my apparent failure? What if it were a test of my heart to reveal my motives for serving him? What if the Lord was disciplining a son he loves (see Heb. 12:6)? If I refused to accept the discipline, I would just have to take the same test over again. There is nothing like a little public humiliation to purify your motives for ministry. I know because I have been experiencing the humiliation ever since I began to pursue prophetic ministry.

No prophet, even the most anointed, ever outgrows the need for a little humiliation now and then. Paul knew that sometimes God might even let the apostles look as though they had failed the test, when, in fact, they had passed it (see 2 Cor. 13:7).

Another discipline all prophetic people have to endure is the "day of small things" (Zech. 4:10). Every prophet would like to be able to tell people the most intimate secrets of their hearts, but most will start out with general words. Nobody starts out as a prophet to the nations. This does not mean God will not use a beginner. One general word that really is from God and given at the right time will have more power than the most profound human insight. Don't despise your humble beginnings. Pursue the Lord more than your ministry, and your future will be prosperous (see Job 8:5-7).

Praying, Practicing, and Risking

Are you satisfied with the level of gifting in your ministry? If not, remember what James said, "You do not have, because you do not ask God" (James 4:2). Pray every day for God to train you in the use of your prophetic gift. Ask him to increase the accuracy of your gift. Ask him for specific things in regard to your prophetic ministry, so you will have a way of measuring whether you are growing in prophecy. Pray for opportunities to use your gift.

Always remember to pray more for the purifying of your character than for the perfecting of your gift. It takes more than a great gift to render great service to God. It takes a great heart. Remember Samson. He did not have the heart to bear his extraordinary physical strength. In the end he lost his strength and his heart to a temptress. I have seen prophets fall to the tempter because they did not have the character to bear their gifts. God gives us gifts, but he requires us to develop the strength of character in order to use those gifts to serve him and not ourselves.

Ask the Lord to send you mentors to help you with your gifting and your character. He has answered this prayer for me by sending me various mentors at different stages of my development, and I cannot exaggerate the important role they have had in my growth. Ask the Lord to make you a mentor to others (see 2 Tim. 2:2), for in teaching and training others, you will grow too.

You can't grow in anything unless you practice. Mature prophets are those "who because of practice have their senses trained to discern good and evil" (Heb. 5:14, NASB). The only good athlete you will ever see is a bad one who refused to give up. So, like an athlete, keep practicing until you acquire the skill you need.

One prophetic friend of mine, Steve Thompson, asks the Lord to speak to him about strangers while he's standing in lines at the bank or grocery store. If he thinks the Lord has spoken to him about a bank teller, he tests it immediately. He asks a harmless, friendly question, "You don't have a sister named Darla, do you?"

"No, why do you ask?"

"Oh, I must have confused you with someone else." No problem. No one but Steve knows he missed it.

But with Steve it would be more likely for her to say, "Yes. How did you know?" Now there is problem because the practice session has just ended, and Steve has to assume that the Lord really wants to say something to this lady. The risk begins, for both of them.

No prophetic word can be judged until it is spoken. But we are such perfectionists. When we were little children, adults told us, "Anything worth doing is worth doing right." They meant well, but they should have told us that we would never do it right without first doing it poorly.

We ask to get the gift, and that takes faith.

We practice to grow in the gift, and that takes discipline.

We risk to bless someone, and that takes courage.

Or we could just play it safe, but then we would never know if we could use the gift when it really counted.

Pray, practice, risk, and find a prophetic community in which you may do all these things.

Prophetic Community

In the Old Testament there were schools of the prophets. Proverbs 13:20 explains why. "He who walks with the wise grows wise, but a companion of fools suffers harm." If we are going to be like the people with whom we choose to fellowship, it follows that we should select our friends wisely. Which is what the Old Testament prophets did. For "as iron sharpens iron, so one man sharpens another" (Prov. 27:17). Being around other prophets will stimulate us to ask questions, cause us to rethink our own experience, allow us to benefit from the experience of those who are more mature, give us faith to grow in our gifting, and motivate us to search the Scriptures more diligently.

The best prophetic community was not the Old Testament schools of prophets but the New Testament church in Antioch, which had both prophets and teachers ministering together (see Acts 13:1-3). Teachers and prophets can benefit from each other's strengths and strengthen each other's weaknesses. The difficulty is finding a church like this. Right now there are not many prophetic churches, schools, or conferences, but there are some that are excellent. It is definitely worth a diligent search to discover them, for the right prophetic environment will help us keep our focus on Jesus, and love one another, and it will protect us from deception. The right prophetic community will also help us learn from our inevitable failures.

Learning From Failure

It is said that nothing succeeds like success. Wise people know that nothing teaches like failure. In every failure there is a new lesson to be learned. The best way *not* to learn from failure is to blame someone else for it. Maybe it was *their* incompetence or lack of character. What about *our* incompetence and *our* lack of character? Maybe the failure lies with us and not others. Personally, I am learning more these days from my own failures and the failures of those close to me than I am from all our successes combined. Let me give you an example.

During my quiet time recently, I received a new (that is, new to me) insight about why marriages grow cold. I saw clearly the various stages of dying love. I also thought I saw a solution for rekindling marital passion. I could not wait for Sunday so I could preach on these new insights. I thought the audience would devour these truths with gratitude.

It didn't happen. Instead, when it was over, my audience looked depressed. I had wanted to inspire hope and transformation, but I had instilled guilt and depression. Why?

The easy solution would have been to blame it on the dullness of the people. But I knew these people. They were not dull. Or I could have blamed the time of year. It was January. Everyone suffers post-Christmas depression in January. Instead of blaming, I simply asked the Lord why the people got depressed after hearing what I thought was a message from him. Almost immediately I got an answer.

It came in complete sentences and went something like this,

"You spent all your time and eloquence describing the death of love. You saved only a few words at the end for its resurrection. If you had reversed this process, the people would have found hope rather than discouragement."

That made perfect sense. An accurate description of death won't save anyone who is dying. A diagnosis does not heal anything. I spent most of my time on the diagnosis rather than on the cure. This failure proved to be one of my greatest blessings in teaching me to use revelatory insights to their full potential.

Here are some texts that have helped focus my attention on me rather than others when I have experienced failure. This has kept me from blaming others, which in turn has kept me from becoming bitter.

Search me, O God, and know my heart;
    test me and know my anxious thoughts.
See if there is any offensive way in me,
    and lead me in the way everlasting.

PSALM 139:23-24

The wisdom of the prudent is to give thought to their ways.

PROVERBS 14:8

A prudent man gives thought to his steps.

PROVERBS 14:15

I applied my heart to what I observed and learned a lesson from what I saw.

PROVERBS 24:32

I have turned these verses into prayers and try to pray them at the beginning of each day. I attach much importance to this because the older I get, the more I realize how blind I am to the real causes of my failures. I have found that when I open my heart to the light of the Lord, he grants me merciful revelations that can turn a setback into a step forward.

At your next revelatory stumble, dust yourself off with the thought that all great spiritual leaders, with one exception, have made great mistakes. Each failure helped them grow a little less confident in themselves and a little more confident in God. What is your latest stumble, and how is it improving you?

Rejoicing in Rejection

It is the occupational hazard of prophets to face rejection. And the greater the gifting, the greater the rejection. It is not the people who first reject the prophet. It is the religious leaders. Jesus, the greatest of all the prophets, was "rejected by the elders, chief priests and teachers of the law" (Mark 8:31). He warned his followers to expect rejection: "Blessed are you when men hate you, when they exclude you and insult you and reject your name as evil, because of the Son of Man. Rejoice in that day and leap for joy, because great is your reward in heaven. For that is how their fathers treated the prophets" (Luke 6:22-23).

Why do religious leaders refuse the ministry of a true prophet? Because the prophet poses a threat to them. God sends prophets to challenge erroneous traditions and to declare new priorities for his people. Leaders of calcified traditions care more about protecting their position than listening to the voice of God. Of course, they don't think of themselves that way.

They think they are defending orthodoxy against the challenges of a radical outsider. You can recognize them by their battle cry: "That's not Presbyterian!" or, "That's not Baptist!" or, "That's not Vineyard!" They act as though God were actually a member of their denomination and wouldn't dream of violating *their* orthodoxy until he had first checked with them.

If the prophet functions at a lower level of anointing, the leadership will easily be able to dismiss him. But if the Spirit powerfully rests on him, they will escalate the rejection to persecution. Leaders will accuse him of being unbiblical, divisive, even demonic. No servant of God has carried a great anointing without having to bear these kinds of accusations.

The place of greatest anointing is also the place of greatest controversy. Think of the controversy that swirled around Jesus, then around the apostles, and, since then, around every major move of God in history. Characteristically in such moves of God, leaders of the reigning orthodoxy have survived for so long by their political skills that they don't even recognize the prophetic anointing they are persecuting.

This persecution is predictable. Jesus told his disciples that enemies would "falsely say all kinds of evil against you because of me" (Matt. 5:11). Too often, sadly, I have seen this prophecy fulfilled. I have listened to Bible-believing leaders spread gross lies and rumors about anointed prophets because they felt some of their constituency might defect to the prophets.

If we get persecuted like this, we're supposed to rejoice. Why?

For one, it may be a sign of the Spirit resting on us in power (Matt. 5:11-12).

Second, rejection and persecution can be great teaching

tools. They purify our motives in ministry and provide us with opportunities to grow in love (see Matt. 5:43-48). I watched Mike Bickle endure the most merciless attack for months. I was amazed by the hatred of his persecutors and by the grace with which Mike bore that hatred, never returning evil for evil. During this time, I did not see any anger eating away at Mike's heart. But the Lord did. He said to Mike, "The measure of your anger toward these men is the measure of your unperceived ambition." Without the persecution, Mike would never have realized his ambition, and how destructive it might have been if not decisively dealt with.

Third, persecution can strengthen ministries by scaring away the people-pleasers. These are people whose highest goal is to please those around them, and, therefore, they cannot be servants of Christ (Gal. 1:10). They are obsessively cautious and constantly worried about offending someone. Rather than endure a confrontation, they will compromise the authority of divine commandments. They weaken a ministry by spreading fear and wasting time initiating unnecessary discussions regarding the ministry's direction. They are usually the first ones to leave when the persecution starts.

Tested by Praise

Praise is a rarer but more difficult test than persecution. The leadership will not normally praise a prophet, but often the people will. They flocked to John the Baptist and to Jesus, praising them both. Because of their strength of character, the praise of the people had no effect on them. With us, though, praise frequently seduces. Whereas rejection may cause us to question ourselves, praise may cause us to feel invulnerable.

Listen to what the wisest of men said about praise: "The crucible for silver and the furnace for gold, but man is tested by the praise he receives" (Prov. 27:21). The greater the prophetic gifting, the greater the testing that will come from praise.

When persecution can't bring us down, and praise can't puff us up, we will have traveled a long way down the road of prophetic maturity. But how does anyone ever get that far?

Prophetic Focus

Prophets have a Counselor to help them keep their focus. Three times Jesus referred to him as "the Spirit of truth." The first context in which the Spirit of truth appears, John 14:15-21, concerns loving and obeying Jesus. The second passage is John 15:26-27, which deals with the Spirit's testimony to Jesus. The last section is John 16:12-16, where the Spirit is said to bring glory to God. The Counselor is called the Spirit of truth because he always points to the Truth, Jesus, and because he reveals the greatest truths to the followers of Jesus. These are the truths that promote the love of Jesus, the testimony of Jesus, and the glory of Jesus. The highest level of prophetic ministry is to be able to consistently discern what promotes these three things.

This means that the ultimate focus of the prophets should never be on their ministries or even on the needs of the people. If prophets want the guidance of the Holy Spirit, they must focus on Jesus because that is where the Holy Spirit is focused. By sharing the focus of the Holy Spirit, we will get to see the glorious, heart-stopping splendor radiating from Jesus.

Persecution, praise, and a thousand other distractions lose their power over us in the presence of his radiant beauty. Everything comes into proper focus when we focus on him. Simple to say, hard to do, and that is one of the reasons that God sends us his prophets, to call us back to that glorious Person who sits at the right hand of the Father, supremely patient as he rules the world by the power of his word and longs to be closer to you and to me.

Enjoying the Symphony

Years ago, when I walked into that dingy room with the green carpet and orange plastic chairs, I had no idea the Word of God was waiting for me. I had no idea of how much inside me needed to be healed, and that only he could heal it. I had no idea of the journey he had planned for me. I had no idea of how much I needed his mercy until I walked into the manger of his mercy.

God's highest purpose for the world was born in a manger. It's been my experience that his highest purposes for you and for me are still being brought to birth in mangers, the places where we least expect to encounter him. The One who lives in the unapproachable light of glory loves to meet us in the most humble of places. Those places become revelations of his humility and his mercy by which he heals us and to which he calls us.

Until that beautiful fall morning, my knowledge of mangers and humility was mainly limited to what I'd read in theological commentaries. And certainly that one prophetic encounter did not make me a deeply humble person nor give me a profound knowledge of God's present-day mangers. But it did give me a little taste for these things, and it caused me to pursue the prophetic ministry from that day on.

Over the years, I have been greatly rewarded by my pursuit. Prophets have helped me with decisions both in my ministry and in my personal life. As a result, my personal life has been more fulfilling and my ministry more fruitful. But these are not the greatest rewards for me.

What I've found most wonderful in the prophets, these agents of God with the otherworldly eyes, is that they are transporters of his mercy. Their eyes see what ours do not. And his mercy heals what our best efforts cannot. My bitterness is gone now, and with it much of the harshness that dogged me for so long. By the light of prophetic words, I can now understand how the events I once viewed as unmitigated disasters fit into the symphony that is my life. Of course, it is an unfinished symphony, but the prophetic trumpets are making it so much richer and stirring.

I don't know the next movement of my own little symphony, but that is fine with me. I am at peace knowing that his mercy will be directing it. The mystery makes the music even more enjoyable.

I do claim, however, to have a little insight about the larger symphony of which all believers are a part and its direction. The prophetic trumpets are growing stronger, announcing a new movement more powerful than anything you or I have ever heard. The new movement won't be heard until the trumpets are well integrated with the rest of the instruments. But that is another story, one that I hope to tell you soon.

RECOMMENDED READING
ABOUT PROPHETIC MINISTRY

From the charismatic tradition:

Growing in the Prophetic, by Mike Bickle (Creation House, 1996).
This book is filled with inspiring stories and a great deal of wisdom for administrating prophecy in the local church.

Prophetic Etiquette, by Michael Sullivant (Creation House, 2000).

The Prophetic Ministry, by Rick Joyner (MorningStar, 1997).
This book has excellent observations on the goal of prophetic ministry and on the character of the prophet.

The Voice of God, by Cindy Jacobs (Regal, 1995, 1997).

You May All Prophesy, by Steve Thompson (MorningStar, 2000).
This book is one of the most helpful on the practical issues of prophetic ministry.

From the Pentecostal tradition:

Prophets and Personal Prophecy, by Bill Hamon (Destiny Image, 1987).

Prophets and the Prophetic Movement, by Bill Hamon (Destiny Image, 1990).

Prophets, Pitfalls, and Principles, by Bill Hamon (Destiny Image, 1991).

From the conservative evangelical tradition:

Surprised by the Voice of God, by Jack Deere (Zondervan, 1996, 1998).

The Gift of Prophecy in the New Testament and Today, by Wayne Grudem (Crossway Books, 1988; due to be reissued in the fall of 2000 with seven new appendices).

Other Books in the *Beginner's Guide* series include:

The Beginner's Guide to Spiritual Warfare,
by Neil T. Anderson and Timothy M. Warner

The Beginner's Guide to Fasting,
by Elmer Towns

The Beginner's Guide to Intercession,
by Dutch Sheets

Ask for them at your nearest Christian bookstore.